SECRETARY'S GUIDE TO CORRECT USAGE, PUNCTUATION, SPELLING AND WORD DIVISION

Theresa M. Reilly

PARKER PUBLISHING COMPANY, INC. West Nyack, N.Y.

Reward Edition . . . . . . September 1982

Library of Congress Cataloging in Publication Data

Reilly, Theresa M
Secretary's guide to correct usage, punctuation, spelling, and word division.

Includes index.
1. Commercial correspondence--Handbooks, manuals, etc. 2. English language--Business English--Handbooks, manuals, etc. I. Title.
HF5726.R42 651.7'402 79-12644
ISBN 0-13-797498-1

Printed in the United States of America

HOW THIS BOOK CAN HELP YOU

This helpful reference book is divded into ten chapters of related information and practical guidelines. A cross-referenced index is included. The central aim in each unit is to provide fast, concise help to the secretary in her transcribing and writing procedures. With the introduction of word-processing equipment into offices, experienced secretaries recognize the need to be alert to correct usage because errors are duplicated in the playback of recorded material. This book will be an invaluable time and effort saver in the constantly changing office scene. The "English of Business" should be direct and to the point; it is concerned with economy of words, and the secretary's role in production is also concerned with this, particularly as it relates to the economy of time.

The first chapter provides you with correct usage, sentence structure and agreement of subject with verb, all designed to convey clear and unadulterated meaning to the reader. Business correspondence is a reflection of the writer, who must be conscious of *What* is said and also *How* it is said. Business people have to be natural in expressing facts and opinions, and their letters should not be faulty in grammar, spelling, or punctuation. While there is no need to edit or compose a letter sticking to the *strictest* rules of grammar and punctuation, business letters need to be clear, concise and correct. A basic assumption is that there are few *absolute* rules in regard to correct usage, and that changes occur according to meaning and use in a sentence. At times it is necessary to make some obviously arbitrary choices of when to use and when to omit punctuation, according to meaning and usage. Chapter 1 increases your ability to construct sentences correctly so that the meaning is clear.

Chapter 2 offers practical tips on English grammar and parts of speech, relative to their use in a sentence. Some aspects of grammar do not have a bearing on usage and composition. Handbooks and dictionaries do not always agree on preferences in grammatical usage, and more than one form may be acceptable in particular instances. In a situation where there are alternatives, once a preference is selected, the element of consistency must prevail. Formal English is utilized in most business letters, legal documents, and certain material for publication. Colloquial expressions are frequently found in friendly business letters. The secretary is not at liberty to change a technical word or even a colloquial expression dictated by a manager. At times, however, she may detect an inadvertent error in grammar; for example, in agreement of subject and verb, because of thought concentration on subject matter by the manager rather than on the mechanics of the language. You may not change an item of substance, but you may correct an accidental error in grammar, provided it does not change the meaning of the dictated material. Chapter 2 offers practical help in expanding the secretary's knowledge and skill in the use of English grammar.

All forms of punctuation are covered in Chapter 3. Punctuation is occasionally debatable, and the trend is toward less punctuation at the informal level. Rules for the comma are not absolute, but relative to usage in making a sentence more readable and readily understandable. The purpose of punctuation is to make meaning clear to the reader. For example, words such as *however* and *therefore* either are or are not preceded or followed by commas according to their use in a sentence. The use of the semicolon or a comma can alter the meaning of a sentence. In Chapter 3 many examples are given illustrating the correct use of the comma, semicolon, colon, and other forms of punctuation, with a view toward helping the secretary to comprehend and to transcribe sentences in a more accurate manner, and to punctuate sentences so that the thought content of the sentence will readily become apparent to the reader.

Chapter 4 illustrates many examples of abbreviations and symbols, in both singular and plural forms, used in titles, published materials, names of persons, companies, and geographical locations. The use of numbers in expressions of time, addresses, money, and various types of data is also included. Recognized authorities do not always agree on matters of style in writing numbers, on the sequential elements denoting chapters, subchapters, and footnotes. In many instances more than one form is acceptable. This chapter represents the majority opinion in writing abbreviations and symbols, and in many instances it indicates that more than one form is acceptable.

Chapter 5 presents the various forms and uses of capitalization with regard to eras, buildings, education, government, business, geographic areas, religion, and various groups of individuals, organizations, and other categories. Different authorities indicate different preferences. When consensus does exist, this chapter will present whatever is the most prevalent form.

Standard and practical guidelines for word division and hyphenation are found in Chapter 6. Illustrative examples are give to complement rules. An incorrectly divided or hyphenated word at the end of a typewritten line leads to stilted reading and inhibits the reader in immediately comprehending the thought content of a sentence or a paragraph. The secretary has constant need for use of word division in the production of attractively typed mailable letters.

Chapter 7 contains a list of the 700 most frequently misspelled words. The words are divided, hyphenated, and accented. The words in this list are not only frequently misspelled, but they are also incorrectly divided in many instances. Also included, with definitions, is a list of words occasionally confused or misused. Chapter 7 will enable the secretary to become quickly familiar with the correct hyphenation and use of words most frequently used in business correspondence.

Chapter 8 illustrates the various styles and components of business letters. In many large firms, office manuals are available to secretaries, and the forms indicated in the manual of a particular company are to be adhered to by all employees. In smaller offices, however, the style of letter may vary according to the preference of the employer or the secretary. Acceptable letter styles prevalent in various business offices are presented in this chapter as a reference for the secretary.

Chapter 9 deals with forms of address and salutation currently used in domestic and foreign situations. Names used are fictitious. At times a choice of possible styles may be indicated. Limitation of space precludes inclusion of all acceptable forms of address and salutation; the omission of any form does not infer that such omitted form is undesirable or incorrect. The forms included here are appropriate, but not necessarily the only acceptable styles. Chapter 9 will serve as a ready reference to acceptable form in the use of styles of address and salutation.

Information that secretaries frequently need in their daily routine is included in Chapter 10. Some of the material is common knowledge and some is information that has recently been developed, changed, or altered in some respect. Inclusion of such pertinent reference material in the final chapter of the *Secretary's Guide to Correct Usage, Punctuation, Spelling and Word Division* will prove a useful and handy source of readily available current information for the secretary.

In summary, this practical guide will enable you to work with ease and confidence in the production of letters, memorandums, and all forms of business correspondence.

Theresa M. Reilly

Also by this Author

Legal Secretary's Word Finder and Desk Book

CONTENTS

How This Book Can Help You 5

1. Acquiring Techniques of Correct Usage in Sentence Structure 13

Developing a sense of sentence completeness using simple, complex, compound, and compound-complex sentences. . . . How to avoid run-on sentences and sentence fragments. . . . Guidelines for use of independent and dependent clauses and the use of prepositional, infinitive, participial, and gerund phrases. . . . Rules for agreement of subject and verb—with compound subjects, correlatives, and subjects in inverted order in sentence. . . . How to use modifiers correctly and effectively.

2. Mastering Rhetoric in Business Communications 25

Identification of parts of speech in their intrinsic forms and relative to their use in a sentence. . . . Illustrative sentences containing nouns. . . . Recognition of various types of pronouns, such as personal, relative, interrogative, demonstrative and indefinite . . . Categories and functions of verbs. . . . Key factors in form and comparison of adjectives and adverbs, including the use of adjective and adverb modifiers. . . . Prepositions and prepositional phrases, with tips on avoiding unnecessary prepositions. . . . How to use subordinate, correlative, and coordinate conjunctions. . . . Developing an understanding of content and structure words. . . . Rhetoric—examples of correct and incorrect usage.

3. Modern Solutions to Punctuation Problems 63

Punctuation at the end of a sentence—when to use the period, question mark, and exclamation point. . . . Practical rules and illustrative material concerning internal punctuation, with rules and illustrations for effective use of the comma, semicolon, and colon. . . . Where to place quotation marks. . . . How to express breaks within a sentence. . . . When to use italics. . . . Rules for the correct placement of the apostrophe. . . . How to use the asterisk, ampersand, and diagonal. . . . Uses of the hyphen with compound adjectives, numbers, locations, and prefixes.

4. Current Usage of Abbreviations and Symbols 93

How to present titles of books, magazines, and newspapers, along with chapters and articles. . . . Manner of indicating case references and citations in legal documents. . . . How to abbreviate names of companies and geographic locations. . . . Guidelines for forming plurals and possessives of abbreviations. . . . Examples of current abbreviations and symbols for time and dates, decimals, fractions, numbers percent, Roman numerals, and data tables.

5. Understanding Forms and Uses of Capitalization 109

Modern methods of expressing names of buildings, geographic areas, eras, groups of individuals, and organizations. . . . How to capitalize and abbreviate degrees in education, medicine, and law. . . . Examples of forms used in national, state, and local governments. . . . Checklist for current business titles and company name forms. . . . Capitalization of religious denominations and holy days, political groups, and holidays.

6. Guidelines for Word Division and Hyphenation 121

Standard rules for dividing words. . . . Illustrative examples complementing rules for hyphenation. . . . Division of words at end of line. . . . Suggestions for forming plurals of compound terms. . . . Practical rules for hyphenating compound terms, prefixes, and suffixes.

7. Simplified Techniques and Rules for Spelling 135

Rules for spelling of words containing combinations of *i* and *e*, words ending in silent *e*, and in *ie*, and for doubling the consonant. . . . Solving difficulties with prefixes *des-* and *dis-*, with suffixes *-able, -ible, -ous, -ance, -ence, -ise,* and *ize*. . . . List of 700 most frequently misspelled words. . . . Combinations of words. . . . Combinations of words occasionally confused or misused.

8. A Practical Guide to Effective Business Letters 185

Suggestions for improving appearance of business letters. . . . Samples of placement of attention line, reference notations, enclosures, and copy indications. . . . Arrangement styles and punctuation of business letters. . . . Estimating length of letter and interoffice memorandum. . . . Placing letters and memorandums attractively. . . . Addressing envelopes for mailing and for interoffice distribution. . . . Models of letters typed in block form and indented form. . . . Format of AMS simplified letter.

9. Forms of Address and Salutation—Domestic and Foreign 217

How to address government officials on the national, state, and local levels. . . . Forms for addressing military personnel, and for clergy of various religious denominations. . . . Forms of address and reference for members of the medical, educational, and legal professions. . . . Foreign equivalents of Mr., Mrs., and Miss. . . . Correct forms of address, salutation, and complimentary close when writing to foreign dignitaries.

10. Essential Reference Data 247

Techniques of report writing. . . . How to set up a report with proper outline sequence, pagination, footnotes, and bibliography. . . . Suggestions for typing minutes of informal and formal business meetings. . . . List of proofreader's marks. . . . Capitals of the United States and of the World. . . . Information relating to dimensions of the Continents, to Arabic figures and Roman numerals. . . . Basic units of the Metric System, common prefixes, metric terms, symbols and equivalents.

Chapter 1

ACQUIRING TECHNIQUES OF CORRECT USAGE IN SENTENCE STRUCTURE

Chapter 1 provides you with helpful data on sentence structure, enabling you to express ideas clearly, correctly, and concisely whether in simple, complex, compound, or more involved sentences. An unusually long sentence containing many descriptive words and phrases may be a simple sentence having one subject and one predicate, yet it has to be correctly constructed in order to convey a clear meaning. In compound and complex sentences having components in forms of descriptive phrases and involved clauses, all modifiers have to be correctly placed in order to give a lucid, intelligible meaning. The illustrative examples used here in identifying each type of setence, phrase, clause, or modifier are basic examples taken from actual business materials. Throughout, information is presented in a clear, concise manner. Hence, the key rules and basic examples are given, rather than options in various aspects of usage involved in many refinements of writing.

A. SENTENCES

1. Style in Grammar

Style means finished and polished sentences. Varied sentences are pleasing. Both the length and the type should be varied. While there are many kinds of sentences in the English language, basically there are four standard types: *simple, complex, compound,* and *complex-compound.*

a. A *simple* sentence contains only one independent clause and no dependent clause.

> The Federal Reserve System was set up by an Act of Congress.
>
> Ability grouping is a controversial subject among administrators and teachers.

Although a sentence may contain many phrases and descriptive words, if it has only one subject and one predicate, it is a SIMPLE sentence.

> In the event of any action or suit, the seller shall have the right to recover any and all expenses and costs of collection, including, without limitation, reasonable attorneys' fees, expenses and disbursements.

b. A *complex* sentence contains one principal clause and one or more subordinate clauses.

> The agreements are in the public interest of the customer, a fact which will be demonstrated at the meeting.
>
> The company submits that its proposed rate for residential service is reasonable and appropriate.

c. A *compound* sentence consists of two or more independent clauses.

The start of crop rotation increased cultivation, and the discovery of chemical fertilizers has led to greater food productivity.

I will be in Chicago during the week of April 10 and I will call you to make an appointment.

d. A *compound-complex* sentence contains at least two principal clauses and one or more subordinate clauses.

After you have had a medical examination, return the application form to us, and we will consider reinstatement of your policy.

Mr. Hale's testimony on the whole, it is submitted, relies too heavily on theory and raises the question whether Mr. Hale is fully familiar with the practical aspects of the situation.

2. Sentence Fragments

A sentence fragment represents an incomplete thought that is incapable of standing alone. In order to be sure that a sentence is complete, find the subject and the predicate.

(Incorrect)	There has been a trend toward establishing chain stores. Especially in the grocery and drug fields.
(Correct)	There has been a trend toward establishing chain stores, especially in the grocery and drug fields.
(Incorrect)	Wishing you success in your new business.
(Correct)	I wish you success in your new business.

3. Run-on Sentences

If a sentence ends with a comma or no punctuation mark and another sentence follows without a capital letter, the error is called a "run-on" or "run-together" sentence.

(Incorrect) When a person applies for a job he may be nervous since an employer is likely to select a person who shows potential in the interview, the applicant should appear confident.

(Correct) When a person applies for a position, he may be nervous. Since an employer is likely to select a person who shows potential in an interview, the applicant should appear confident.

(Incorrect) In a company manual form letters are classified according to subject, then each letter is coded for easy reference.

(Correct) In a company manual, form letters are classified according to subject. Then each letter is coded for easy reference.

4. Clauses

A clause contains a subject and a predicate. Clauses may be independent or dependent.

a. Independent

An independent or principal clause can stand alone; in effect, it is a simple sentence.

b. Dependent

A dependent or subordinate clause begins with a subordinating connective and depends on the rest of the sentence. A dependent clause is used like an *adjective*, an *adverb*, or a *noun*.

(1) An *adjective* clause modifies a noun or a pronoun. It usually begins with one of the following relative pronouns: *who*, *whom*, *whose*, *which*, or *that*.

My brother, *who* is a well-known attorney, has an office in the Madison Building.

Many people for *whom* weight is a problem are now following a stay-thin diet.

Equal opportunity laws have helped women *whose* former attitudes and upbringing had given them little impetus to enter the labor market.

A house organ is a publication *which* contains information of interest to a particular organization.

He stated *that* under the provisions of the Lien Law this is a preferred claim for the amount due.

(2) An *adverb* clause begins with a subordinate conjunction which expresses a relationship between the adverb clause and some other idea.

When a person purchases an automobile, he usually wants delivery as soon as possible.

Because minutes of a corporation are important, notes should be made of all business transacted at a meeting.

(3) A *noun* clause is used as a noun. It begins with a relative pronoun or with a subordinating conjunction.

The end results of business activity are the goods and services that customers use to satisfy their needs and wants.

A personnel manager notes how an applicant walks into his office.

5. Phrases

A phrase is a group of words not having a subject and a predicate. There are six kinds of phrases: *prepositional*, *infinitive*, *participial*, *gerund*, *verb*, and *absolute*.

a. Prepositional—preposition plus an object:

Most professional organizations have some kind *of publications program.*

b. Infinitive—infinitive plus an object:

George wanted *to read the newspaper.*

c. Participial—participle plus an object:

He watched the dog *running down the street.*

d. Gerund—gerund plus an object:

Installing electronic equipment will cost the company thousands of dollars.

e. Verb—complete verb:

They *should have read* the regulations.

f. Absolute—words modifying a clause or a sentence as a whole but not linked to it by a conjunction or a relative pronoun:

As a point of reference, changes in the nature and functions of office work have been brought about by the electronic computer.

B. AGREEMENT OF SUBJECT AND VERB

For a sentence to be correct, the verb must agree in number with the subject.

1. Nouns as Subjects

Certain types of nouns cause problems in subject-verb agreement.

a. Collective Nouns

A collective noun takes a singular verb when the *group* is implied and a plural verb when the individuals are implied.

The *Board is* meeting in the conference room.

The *Committee have* not agreed on the disposition of the property.

b. Singular Nouns Plural in Form

Nouns that are plural in form but singular in meaning take singular verbs.

Politics is a challenging profession.

Sixty miles per hour is the speed limit on many highways.

Fifty dollars is the price I paid for my sport coat.

Four to seven years is the period required for certificates of deposit earning 7½% interest.

Seven pounds is a good weight for a new-born baby.

c. Noun Phrases

The *simple subject* of a noun phrase determines whether the verb will be singular or plural.

An abandoned *building* with broken doors *was* the boys' hideout.

A *list* of volunteers *is* maintained in the main office.

2. Pronouns as Subjects

a. Relative Prounouns

When a relative pronoun is the subject, the verb agrees in number with its antecedent. The antecedent is usually the noun or pronoun immediately preceding the relative pronoun.

Bob is one of those boys *who do* well in all athletic games. ["boys" and not "one" is the antecedent]

I do not know the woman *who is* calling you. ["woman" is the antecedent]

b. Indefinite Pronouns

The indefinite pronouns *one, each, either,* and *neither* require singular verbs.

Either the president or the vice-president is present at every meeting.

Neither Evans nor Brown fears the verdict.

The indefinite pronouns *any* and *none* may take either a singular or a plural verb.

Any of the players *is* (or *are*) entitled to challenge the decision.

None of you is (or *are*) responsible.

3. Compound Subjects

Two or more subjects joined by *and* form a plural subject and take a plural verb:

Bill and his *friends are coming* for dinner on Sunday.

When two nouns are considered as a single idea, they take a singular verb:

Ham and eggs is on the breakfast menu.

4. Correlatives

When compound subjects are joined by correlatives: *either . . . or, neither . . . nor, not only . . . but also,* the verb agrees with the part of the compound nearer it.

Neither the girls nor *Helen was* on time.

Either Nancy or *you are* holding the book.

Not only Dick but also his *sons are* enjoying the game.

All the boys but not a single *girl was* interested in the movie.

5. Subjects in Inverted Order in Sentence

If a subject follows the verb, the verb still agrees in number with the subject.

Among the exhibitors at the antique show *are a number of dealers* from New England.

A most unusual antique *is* a double-bonnet top *bureau* of mulberry wood, which is a bit darker than walnut.

6. Modifiers

A modifier is a word or a group of words that describes or clarifies another word or group. By using modifiers correctly and effectively, ideas can be clearly and well expressed.

a. Adjective:

Specialty shops have maintained *effective* competition through their resourcefulness and the ingenuity of their owners or buyers.

[Adjective modifiers modify a noun or a pronoun.]

b. Adverb:

The pioneers moved *westward,* their caravans proceeding *cautiously* and going no *faster* than the family cow.

[Adverb modifiers modify an adjective, a verb, or another adverb.]

c. Phrase:

The available literature *on industrial hygiene* is very vast.

d. Clause:

Soaring prices for fruit and vegetable crops, *which were damaged by the winter freeze,* gave a new push to inflation.

e. Sentence:

Under the circumstances, we should engage in plea bargaining.

[If a modifier modifies an entire idea, it is a sentence modifier.]

f. Misplaced Modifier:

Wrong: Evelyn was told that her work was entirely satisfactory by the personnel manager.

Right: Evelyn was told by the personnel manager that her work was entirely satisfactory.

[When a modifier is *misplaced,* it is not clear which word or group of words is modified.]

g. Misused Modifier:

Wrong: After Philip returned from Europe, he gambled considerable.

Right: After Philip returned from Europe, he gambled considerably.

[Misused modifier is the incorrect use of an adjective for an adverb to modify a verb, and the incorrect use of an adverb as a predicate adjective.]

Wrong: Nick seems to think different now.

Right: Nick seems to think differently now.

h. Dangling Modifier:

Wrong: Without sturdy boots the storm could not be weathered.

Right: Without sturdy boots he could not weather the storm.

[A *dangling* modifier has no word or group of words to modify.]

SUMMARY

Chapter 1 presented the elements of correct usage principally with regard to sentence structure. Included in the material were illustrative examples of complete sentences, samples of run-on sentences, sentence fragments, various types of clauses, phrases, and modifiers. Reference was made to the agreement of subject and verb with regard to simple and compound subjects, correlatives, and subjects in inverted order in a sentence.

Chapter 2

MASTERING RHETORIC IN BUSINESS COMMUNICATIONS

The world of business constantly provides opportunities for the exercise of the arts of observation, listening, reading, and reasoning; the arts of comparison, classification, distinction, relation, and order; and particularly the arts of expression and communication. Successful businessmen must have knowledge of rhetoric—the effective and meaningful use of words. Correct use of English is central to both oral and written communication.

A. PARTS OF SPEECH

Each word in our language is a part of speech and has a characteristic form and function. Words are grouped into eight parts of speech: *nouns*, *pronouns*, *verbs*, *adjectives*, *adverbs*, *prepositions*, *conjunctions*, and *interjections*. The parts of speech that constitute the mainspring of meaning in our language are known as content words: *nouns*, *verbs*, *adjectives*, and *adverbs*. These words make up approximately 99 percent of all words listed in the dictionary. *Pronouns* are personal or relative and are used with reference to persons, animals, places, and things. *Prepositions* are classified as function or structure words; they connect and relate other parts of speech. *Conjunctions* function as connectors and are classified as coordinate or subordinate. *Interjections* are exclamations and may be followed either by an exclamation mark or a comma.

Prepositions, conjunctions, and *interjections* never change their form.

Certain parts of speech change their form to show specific meaning or grammatical relationship to other words or group of words. Such change is classified as *inflection:*

Inflection of *nouns* and *pronouns* is called *declension;*
Inflection of *verbs* is called *conjugation;*
Inflection of *adjectives* and *adverbs* is called *comparison.*

Nouns change form to indicate *number* and *case:*

		Possessive	
Singular	*Plural*	*Singular*	*Plural*
boy	boys	boy's	boys'
lady	ladies	lady's	ladies'
child	children	child's	children's
man	men	man's	men's

Pronouns change form to indicate *person, number,* or *case:*

I—me, my, mine	someone—someone's
we—us, our, ours	this, that
who—whom, whose	these, those
he—him, his	
she—her, hers	
they—them, theirs	

Verbs change form to indicate *tense, person, number,* or *mood:*

take, takes	took	taking	taken
bake, bakes	baked	baking	baked
lie, lies	lay	lying	lain
lay, lays	laid	laying	laid
be, am, is, are	was, were	being	been
drink, drinks	drank	drinking	drunk

Adjectives and *adverbs* change form to indicate *comparison* or *number:*

good	better	best
many	more	most
bad	worse	worst
little	less	least
quick	quicker	quickest
lively	livelier	liveliest
far	farther	farthest

Each part of speech is discussed and illustrated more extensively under its respective heading in this chapter.

1. Nouns

A noun is the name of any person, animal, place, thing, or idea: man, dog, town, desk, or love. Nouns are often preceded by one of the indefinite articles *a* or *an;* by the definite article *the;* or by a possessive word such as *her, his, my, our, your, its,* etc.

a. Nouns can be *singular, plural,* or *possessive.* A noun usually changes form to indicate the plural and the possessive case:

The *Jones* family is happy.

All the *Joneses* are going to Europe to celebrate Mr. and Mrs. *Jones'* (or *Jones's*) Twenty-Fifth Wedding Anniversary.

b. Certain word endings are *noun-forming suffixes:*

advise + ment	=	advisement
appear + ance	=	appearance
apply + ication	=	application
author + ity	=	authority
defend + ant	=	defendant

depend + ent	=	dependent
notify + ication	=	notification
object + ive	=	objective
present + ation	=	presentation
refer + ence	=	reference
refer + endum	=	referendum
retire + e	=	retiree

c. Types of Nouns:

Common—a lake, an animal, the sea
proper—Chicago, Madison Square Garden, Mrs. George Fulton
concrete—a pen, an orange, an automobile, the train
abstract—friendship, awareness, integrity, fear
collective—a quorum, the committee, fruit, an assembly
count—five cents, data, many questions
mass—monies, crowd, media, army

d. Compound Nouns:

Regardless of spelling, the first part of the compound is usually stressed:

blacktop, breakfast, dropout, mother-in-law, watchman, watermain, watermelon.

2. Pronouns

Pronouns have property of person, number, gender, and case; and may be used in first, second, or third person. They are singular or plural in number; masculine, feminine, or neuter in gender; nominative, possessive, or objective in case. Pronouns are classified as follows:

a. Personal Pronouns

Case	*Singular*	*Plural*
Nominative	I	we
	you	you
	he, she, it	they

Possessive	my, mine	our, ours
	your, yours	your, yours
	his, her, hers, its	their, theirs
Objective	me	us
	you	you
	him, her, it	them

(1) The singular possessive form of *yours*, *hers*, and *its*, and the plural possessive form of *ours*, *yours*, and *theirs* do not require an apostrophe.

(2) Personal pronouns also have *reflexive* forms:

myself	ourselves
yourself	yourselves
himself, herself,	themselves
& itself	themselves

(3) Personal pronouns must agree in number with their antecedents:

The *committee* votes on the program *it* approves. (singular)

The *committee* cast *their* votes after discussion of the topic. (as individuals)

The mother and her *children* enjoyed *their* picnic. (plural)

(4) When the antecedent involves persons of both sexes, the *masculine* personal pronoun is used:

Everyone minds *his* own business.

b. Relative Pronouns

Nominative	*Possessive*	*Objective*
who	whose	whom
which	whose	which
what	—	—
that	whose	that

Note: *Who* refers to *persons*
Which refers to *things*

That to *persons* or *things; that* is used when referring to animals, with collective nouns, and when both persons and things are concerned.

c. Interrogative Pronouns. Who and *whom* are classified as interrogative pronouns.

d. Demonstrative Pronouns are: *this, that, these* and *those.*

e. Indefinite Pronouns are singular in *form.* They *function* as nouns but make indefinite reference to people and things:

one	anybody	other
anyone	everybody	another
everyone	nobody	each other
someone	somebody	one another
no one		

The word "else" is used as follows:

anyone else, someone else, no one else, anybody else, everybody else, nobody else, and somebody else.

(2) *Possessive case.* The possessive case is used where the pronoun shows ownership.

Her claim was processed immediately.

Can we depend on *your* doing accurate work?

Whose papers are on the desk?

(3) *Objective case.* The objective case is used in the following instances:

(a) When a pronoun is the object of a *verb* or *preposition:*

An employer should employ *whomever* he considers to be the most qualified. (object of verb *considers*)

The argument was between you and *me.* (object of preposition *between*)

(b) When a pronoun is the subject of an *infinitive.*

Whom are you waiting to see? (object of *infinitive phrase* to see)

3. Verbs

Verbs are words that express action or state of being. *Tense* indicates the time of occurrence of the action or state of being:

The ship *is* sailing.
The ship *will* sail tomorrow.

Verbs are identified by *form.* Most verbs end in *s* or *es* for the present tense third person singular:

He (she) acts. He (she) goes. He (she, it) takes.

Verbs always end in *ing* in their present participle form:

acting, going, taking, running, making, writing, etc.

The past participle of *regular* verbs is formed by adding *d* or *ed* to the basic form:

loved, baked, acted, substituted, etc.

For *irregular* verbs, the past tense and past participle forms are varied:

Present	*Past*	*Present Participle*	*(preceded by has, have, had) Past Participle*
go, goes	went	going	gone
am, are, is	was, were	being	been
think, thinks,	thought	thinking	thought
do, does	did	doing	done

break, breaks	broke	breaking	broken
take, takes	took	taking	taken

Note: Verb forms are more fully discussed in Section B of this Chapter 2, which deals with the parts of speech relative to use in sentences.

a. Categories of Verbs

Verbs are divided into three categories: intransitive, transitive, and linking.

(1) An *intransitive* verb does not require a direct object to complete its meaning:

The guest *has been waiting* in the reception hall. Rosemary *smiled* at the boss. ["in the reception hall" and "at the boss" are modifiers, not direct objects.]

(2) *A* transitive verb takes a direct object; the action is performed on someone or something:

Jack *smokes* king-size cigarettes. (Direct object: cigarettes)

(3) *Linking* verbs relate the subject to the subject complement; they are state-of-being verbs: *be, is, become, appear, feel.* Linking verbs are followed either by a predicate noun or a predicate adjective:

She *is* an attorney.

The ocean *appears* calm.

The paper *feels* smooth.

The assessments *are becoming* excessive.

b. Functions of Verbs

Verbs function according to tense, voice, or mood.

(1) *Tense* specifies time of occurrence: present, past, or future:

Present: Premises selling food *must meet* all City regulations.

Past: The resolution *made* provisions for contributions.

Future: Employees of affiliated institutions *will become* participants in benefits.

(2) *Voice* is concerned with whether a subject acts or is acted upon. Only action verbs have voice.

Active voice (subject performs action):

The company *contributes* to the retirement plan.

Passive voice (subject receives action):

The residents *were disturbed* by the loud music and conversations.

Note: It is incorrect to use *active* and *passive* voice in the same sentence.

(3) *Mood* is the form of the verb which indicates the speaker's attitude towards the factuality of what he says. The English language has three moods: *indicative, subjunctive,* and *imperative.*

(a) The *indicative* mood is used in making statements or asking questions:

The Court *informed* us that the trial would take place on Monday.

Will the defendant be present?

(b) The *subjunctive* mood is used to express a wish or condition contrary to fact, or doubt, and other nonfactual concepts. It is also used in "that" clauses of request or recommendation.

I wish I were a member of the organization.

Sam wishes he were in Alaska.

If the lease be in order, please execute it.

If I were you, I would not invest in that stock.

The president recommended that the rules be changed.

(c) The *imperative* mood is used to state a command, make a request, or to give directions:

Close the door.

Please mail this letter.

Turn left at the next traffic light.

c. Complements of Verbs

A complement is a word or words used to complete the sense of the verb and structure of the predicate, the subject, or the object.

(1) *Object with transitive verb*

Mr. Moore gave his wife a gift of common stock.
[*gift* is the direct object; *wife* is the indirect object.]

(2) *Subject complement with linking verb*

The speaker is *persuasive.*
[*persuasive* is a *predicate adjective* complementing the *subject* speaker.]

Mrs. Monroe is a competent *supervisor.*
[*supervisor* is a *predicate noun* and refers to the *subject,* Mrs. Monroe.]

(3) *Object complement* is used with such words as: *appoint, elect, name, nominate, make, paint.*

They appointed Bruce chairman.
[The noun *chairman* refers to Bruce, the direct object.]

Her father painted the barn *red.*
[The adjective *red* modifies the direct object barn.]

d. Nonfinite Verbs

A nonfinite verb is a verb that cannot stand as the only verb in a sentence. A nonfinite verb (a verbal) may function as a noun, an adjective, or an adverb. *Verbals* have the characteristics of verbs and may take complements, modifiers, objects, and occasionally a subject. Three types of verbals or nonfinite verbs are: *gerunds*, *participles*, and *infinitives*.

(1) A *gerund* is a nonfinite verb that ends in *ing* and functions as a noun. Gerunds take objects, complements, or modifiers:

The robber escaped by *jumping* frantically.
[*jumping* is the object of the preposition *by* and is modified by the adverb frantically.]

Rowing a boat is good exercise.
[gerund = rowing; object = boat; gerund phrase is the subject of the sentence.]

Your going to the office with me is a great service.
[*Your* may be classified as an adjectival modifying the gerund *going*; *Your going* is the subject of the verb *is*.]

Note: A noun or a pronoun modifying a gerund is always in the possessive case.

(2) A *participle* is a verb form that may function as part of a verb phrase, as an adjective, or as a nonfinite verb.

Verb phrase:	The office boy *has finished* delivering the mail.
Adjective:	The *finished* report has the approval of the board of directors.
Nonfinite verb:	Mark, *running* quickly to the files, discovered they were closed. [participle *running* is modified by the adverb *quickly* and by the prepositional phrase *to the files;* the participial phrase modifies *Mark.*]

Nonfinite verb:	The waiter, *carrying* a heavy load of dishes, slipped on the floor. [*carrying* takes the object *load;* the entire participial phrase modifies *waiter.*]

(3) An *infinitive* is a nonfinite verb used principally as a noun and sometimes as an adjective or an adverb. It is made up of the word *to* plus the present form or stem of a verb. Infinitives have subjects, complements, objects, or modifiers.

Subject:	*To forget* and *to forgive* apparent wrongs is a constant struggle.
Complement:	A good thing *to remember* is that the most expensive item is often the cheapest in the end.
Object:	I told him *to shut* the window.
Adjective modifier:	The amount of work *to be done* is overwhelming.
Adverbial modifier:	*To say* the least, this is an outstanding performance.

The object of a *nonfinite verb* is any noun or its substitute that completes the meaning of a participle, a gerund, or an infinitive.

e. Finite Verbs

A finite verb can stand alone and can serve as the only verb of a sentence or a clause. Verbals such as gerunds, participles, and infinitives are not finite verbs.

Verb alone:	Think!
Simple sentence:	He thinks.

The object of a finite verb is any noun or word used as a noun that answers the question *What?* or *Whom?* after a transitive active verb.

David *operates* the duplicating *machines*.

Mr. Coffey *knows* the *president* very well.

f. Coined Verbs

Coined verbs may be used in the present, past, or participle form:

Will you please OK this charge?

He X'd out one item.

Sam is Xeroxing the agreement forms.

While OK'ing the invoice, she discovered an error.

g. Contiguous Verbs

When one verb directly follows another, use a comma between the verbs:

Whenever you sing, sing softly and clearly.

Whatever you do, do not give up trying.

h. Omitted Verbs

In parallel construction, verbs are often implied, and their omission is indicated by a comma:

Lord's Specialty Shop sells blouses; Hayne's Shop, shoes; and Grant's Specialty Shoppe, lingerie.

i. Verbal Phrases

A verbal phrase consists of a verb form plus other words used to form a unit.

The person *to see about passes* is Mr. Jerome.

Recognizing that we were in a traffic jam, we had to be patient.

Swimming every day helps keep me in good health.

Known for her tasty omelets, Maude became a successful restaurant owner.

j. Misuse of Verbs

Errors in the use of verbs sometimes result from the unnecessary use of a particle with a verb, or the use of an incorrect verb form or auxiliary.

(1) *Particle with verb* consists of the use of an uninflected word following a verb; the result is a grammatically incorrect sentence.

Incorrect	*Correct*
Where's he at?	Where is he?
They ran out on us.	They deserted us.
I will not put up with such nonsense.	I will not tolerate such nonsense.
His father cut him off from his will.	His father disinherited him. *or* His father left him nothing.
He fell off of the log.	He fell off the log.
I could of been at the beach.	I could have been at the beach

(2) *Irregular* verbs present difficulty in correct usage; the right verb must be chosen and used with the correct *auxiliary* verb if one is needed. The following auxiliary verbs are used with the present and past participle: *is, are, was, were, been; has, have, had; could, should, and would.*

Gerald Horne *is going* to join our firm.

Two clients *are waiting* in the reception room.

The cows *are lying* (not *laying*) on the grass.

The president of the bank *was talking* with the treasurer.

The officers *were considering* the new proposals.

Many changes *have been made* in federal bank holding company laws in the past few years.

Avery Fisher Hall *has opened* its doors to music with sounds superbly blended.

Several states *have adopted* rules for mandatory continuing education for school dropouts.

A number of people *had reserved* space on the special flight to Japan.

An accountant *could have estimated* the expenses for traveling.

The motorist *should have had* adequate insurance to cover the accident.

A knowledge of sailing regulations *would have helped* some contestants in the race.

Errors in verb usage, as well as misuse of other words, frequently result from failure to recognize meaning of words that are similar in sound but different in spelling. A sample listing of such words appears on pages 160 to 184 in Chapter 7.

4. Adjectives

Adjectives modify or qualify nouns and pronouns (or gerunds) and are generally placed near the words they modify. The articles *a*, *an*, and *the* are classified as adjectives or function words.

a. Uses of Adjectives

(1) An adjective is used to describe the *quality* or *condition* of the subject:

The *view* from the mountain is *beautiful.*

A *reasonable solution* should be forthcoming.

The word *number* preceded by *a* takes a plural verb; when preceded by *the*, the word *number* takes a singular verb:

A number of people *are* coming to the meeting.

The number of persons in attendance at the recital *was* small.

(2) An adjective denotes quality or condition of the subject with verbs of the *senses* and *copulative* verbs:

(a) Verbs of the *senses:*

The dessert *tasted* delicious.

The pine trees *smell* good.

The buzzer *sounds* loud.

He *looks* happy.

I *feel* great.

(b) *Copulative* verbs:

There *is* an easy way to solve that problem.

Brad *seems* delighted with his new office.

Difficult tasks *become* lighter as time goes on.

She *appears* interested.

(3) An adjective denotes the *quality or condition of the object:*

The secretary telephoned to remind him of the *directors'* meeting

The buyer ordered *cotton* dresses.

(4) *Possessive pronouns as adjectives.* Pronouns in their

possessive forms are used as adjectives to modify *nouns* and *gerunds*.

Modifying nouns:

Your display of toys is attractive.

I admire *his patience.*

My pen is fine.

The board enjoyed holding *its meeting* in the new conference room.

Modifying gerunds:

Is there any possibility of *their buying* a house in Chicago?

Her studying the situation proved beneficial.

The employees of the subsidiary resented *our taking* over the company.

His leaving the firm was a surprise to us.

b. Form of Adjectives

Some words have the same form whether used as adjectives or adverbs:

far	The building is a *far* cry from its former condition. (adjective)
	Sales for the current year are running *far* ahead of last year. (adverb)
fast	Susan is a *fast* and accurate typist. (adjective)
	My watch seems to run *fast.* (adverb)
first	You will be the *first* to know. (adjective)
	First, you have to plug in the machine. (adverb)

c. Comparison of Adjectives

At times the adjective is difficult to identify since other parts of speech, such as nouns and verbs, also carry elements of description. An understanding of the characteristics of adjectives should help in identifying them. Almost all adjectives can be compared: The *comparative* degree is used when comparing two persons or things, and is used with *er* or *more* for regular verbs; the *superlative* degree is used when comparing more than two persons or things, and is used with *est* or *most* for regular verbs.

	Stem	*Comparative*	*Superlative*
Regular	cool	cooler	coolest
	rapid	more rapid	most rapid

Wednesday was the *coolest* day this week.

The train is more *rapid* than the boat.

Irregular	bad	worse	worst
	good	better	best

The roads are *worse* today.

This is the *best* solution.

Exceptions. Certain adjectives have an element of completeness and usually are not compared, such as:

considerable	fundamental	superb
deliberate	infallible	unbelievable
excellent	intrinsic	unique
exorbitant	perfect	winsome

d. Adjectivals

Any word or word group that modifies a noun or a pronoun functions as an *adjectival.* The following are examples:

We can no longer tolerate the *negative* attitude and *resulting* delays that occur because of defects in *your construction* work.

A boy *wearing a baseball hat* delivered the package.

Being exhausted Dick decided to retire for the evening.

Dr. Cook, *whose specialty is cardiology,* is at the Madison Hospital.

e. Use of a *and* an

Use the indefinite article *a* before words in which the first sound is a consonant, a sounded *h,* or a long *u:*

a desk
a cabinet

a history book
a hotel
a husband

a union card
a unanimous decision

Use the article *an* before words in which the first sound is a vowel (except long *u*) and before words beginning with silent *h:*

an envelope
an automatic typewriter

an hourly rate
an honorarium

f. Use of a, an, *and* the

The adjectives (or articles) *a, an,* and *the* should be repeated in referring to two separate persons or objects:

The position was open to either *a* man or *a* woman. (two persons)

I have *a* desk and *a* typewriter. (two objects)

He is *a* vice president and general manager. (one person)

I have *a* blue and beige suit. (one suit)

When two or more nouns refer to the same person, the article should not be repeated:

Henry Brooks Adams was *a* historian, writer, and teacher.

Machiavelli was *a* statesman and writer.

g. Agreement of Adjective and Noun

(1) This and *that* are singular and must be used to modify singular nouns.

This kind (not *these* kind) of car is strong.

That type (not *those* type) of duplicating machine is productive.

(2) *These* and *those* are plural and must be used to modify plural nouns.

These kinds of cars are strong.

Those types of duplicating machines are productive.

h. Proper Adjectives

A proper adjective is a descriptive adjective derived from a proper noun. Proper adjectives are capitalized unless they have lost their association with the nouns from which they were derived: American literature, German mark, Italian opera, *but* macadamized road, china silk, pasteurized milk, french fries.

5. Adverbs

An adverb is a word used to modify a verb, an adjective, or another adverb. An *adverb explains* the action of a verb:

The candidates *answered* the questions *clearly* and *distinctly.*

a. Position of Adverbs in Sentences

An adverb should usually be placed as near as possible to the word it modifies. The *position of an adverb* affects the meaning of the sentence.

Do you recall *ever receiving* the letter? (not: ever recall.)

He saw *only* one person. (not: only saw)

She nominated *only* Mr. Baker for chairman. (She did not nominate any other person.)

She *only* nominated Mr. Baker for chairman. (She did not vote for him.)

(1) The adverb should be placed before the participle when it modifies the participle only:

The project has been *successfully* completed.

(2) The adverb is usually placed between the parts of a compound verb:

The shareholders will *undoubtedly* be pleased with the report.

(3) An adverb should not split an infinitive:

He found it difficult *to provide adequately* for his wife and children. (not: to adequately provide)

An adverb is placed first in a sentence when it qualifies the whole sentence or when it is used emphatically:

Fortunately no one was injured in the accident.

Greatly to his surprise, he was selected among 150 applicants.

Certainly John Quinn radiates good will.

b. Adverbial Forms

Some words have two adverbial forms: *slow, slowly; direct; directly; cheap, cheaply,* and others.

Drive *slow.*

Go *slowly* around the curves.

Please send the check *direct* to me.

They will proceed *directly* to the court.

You can buy cars *cheap* on the north side of town.

The suits were *cheaply* made.

c. Adverbial Modifiers

Adverbial modifiers may be words, phrases, or clauses. They indicate condition or assertion, manner (how), time (when), place (where), degree (how much), and cause (why).

(1) *Adverbs* modifying a *verb:*

The coat fits her *snugly* and *perfectly.*

(2) *Adverbs* modifying an *adjective:*

The *very* young man has a *reasonably* secure future.

(3) *Adverbs* modifying another *adverb:*

Don walks *too* fast and Eve walks *exceptionally* slow.

(4) *Infinitive phrase used as an adverb:*

The man came *to repair the telephone.*

(5) *Adverb clause:*

When Mr. Brown finished reading the paper, he dictated letters.

d. Conjunctive Adverbs.

In addition to being modifiers, adverbs may serve as conjunctions connecting two independent clauses of a compound sentence. Some of the common conjunctive adverbs are: *hence, therefore, thus, moreover, however, furthermore, so, accordingly, nevertheless, yet, consequently.*

Punctuation in sentences containing conjunctive adverbs varies according to the use of the adverb. The most common punctuation, however, is that the conjunctive adverb be preceded with a semicolon and followed by a comma:

> Production of the new equipment is proceeding well; nevertheless, the quantity is insufficient at this time.
>
> However unfavorable the weather may be, I shall keep my appointment in the West.
>
> You will note, however, that I have corrected the statement in three places.
>
> It is difficult to know for whom to vote; therefore, I shall study the issues more carefully.

e. Double Negatives

Two negative statements should not be used in the same sentence in order to express a single negative:

Correct	*Incorrect*
I cannot find it anywhere.	I cannot find it nowhere.
She cannot go any place.	She cannot go no place.
Grace could hardly see the house through the fog.	Grace couldn't hardly see the house through the fog.
He won't get any money for that old car.	He won't get no money for that old car.

f. Confusing Adjectives with Adverbs

The *-ly* ending nearly always converts adjectives to adverbs:

> He feels *bad.* (ill)
> He handled the transaction *badly.* (carelessly or offensively)
>
> This is a *real* problem.
> This *really* is a problem.

It was a *slow* bus.
The plane was *slowly* circling over the field.

This is a *rare* specimen.
People *rarely* see the same movie twice.

g. Comparison of Adverbs

Like adjectives, most adverbs have three degrees of comparison: positive, comparative and superlative.

	Positive	*Comparative*	*Superlative*
Regular	early	earlier	earliest
	fast	faster	fastest
Irregular	much, many	more	most
	badly	worse	worst
adverbs	boldly	more boldly	most boldly
ending in	easily	less easily	least easily
-ly	sincerely	more sincerely	most sincerely

h. Common Errors in Use of Adverbs

Among the common errors in the use of adverbs are the interchange of adverbs and adjectives, misuse of comparative forms, and addition of inappropriate words in a sentence.

(1) She is a pianist of *real* skill. (*real* is an adjective of quality)

It is *very* (or *really,* not *real*) cold today. (*very* is an adverb of degree)

(2) She feels *bad.* (ill) (adjective)

He is a *bad* (wicked) person. (adjective)

The child behaves *badly.* (in an offensive manner) (adverb) [*bad means ill, wicked, sorry, offensive; badly* means in an offensive or incompetent manner.]

(3) He had no sooner left *than* (not *when*) she called. [Phrase *no sooner* is followed by *than,* not *when*.]

(4) She is extremely (not *awfully*) clever.
[The adjective *awful* or the adverb *awfully* should not be used for *very, really, extremely.*]

(5) Bill is *somewhat* (not *some*) taller than Dick.

(6) She would like a *different* type of house. (adjective)

He should have signed the paper *differently.* (adverb)

(7) [*Unnecessary* adverbs should be avoided:]

Each page of the manuscript should be *numbered* (not *numbered throughout*).

Finish (not *finish up*) the work.

She *repeated* (not *repeated again*) the name.

They *divided* (not *divided up*) the money.

6. Prepositions

A preposition is a connecting word that shows the relationship between two words. The second word is usually a noun or pronoun which functions as the object of the prepositional phrase:

> We enclose a copy *of our catalog in which* you will find described our complete line *of camping equipment.*

a. Prepositional Phrases

A prepositional phrase consists of the preposition, its object, and all modifiers. Prepositional phrases are used as adjectival or adverbial modifiers. Adjective prepositional phrases are placed after the nouns or pronouns they modify. Adverb prepositional phrases are placed at the beginning of a sentence, after intransitive verbs, or after direct objects of a transitive verb.

> We can refer you *to an attorney* who will take care *of your problem.*
> (Prepositional phrases used as adjectives modifying pronoun *you* and noun *care.*)

After the new payroll increase is known, the company should be allowed to file increased rates designed to recover higher payroll costs.
(Prepositional phrase used as an adverb at the beginning of a sentence.)

Businessmen read *on the train* each morning.
(Prepositional phrase used as an adverb and placed after intransitive verb *read*.)

They read newspapers *on the train.*
(Prepositional phrase used as an adverb and placed after the direct object *newspapers.*)

b. Preposition Ending a Sentence

A preposition may follow rather than precede its object, and it may be placed at the end of a sentence. Formerly it was considered poor usage to end a sentence with a preposition, but it is now often the natural word order since a sentence may become clumsy by avoidance of a preposition at the end.

What are you looking for?

What does he want that for?

Faith, hope, and love are what we live by.

How much are you selling it for?

c. Unnecessary Prepositions

Frequently prepositions are unnecessarily added to verbs that already convey an idea; such prepositions result in incorrect usage. The italicized words are unnecessary.

The hearing will be held at the Courthouse *at about* eight o'clock. (Use either word, not both.)

Where is the boss *at*?

When are you going to start *in* working on my car?

Do not eat *up* all the dessert.

Please call me *up* when you have the answer.

His hat blew off *of* his head.

She took the paper off *from* his desk.

d. Idiomatic Use of Prepositions

Prepositions are structure words, not content words. Most prepositions do have some meaning, but the selection of the correct preposition to follow a verb is sometimes difficult; for example:

He is	*at* the store	*in* the store
	at the telephone	*on* the telephone
	talking *with*	talking *to*

The use of many prepositions is idiomatic; that is, there is no logical reason for their choice, and they are accepted because of prevailing usage. Listed below are some examples of idiomatic uses:

adapted for	The convertible is adapted for sleeping and sitting.
adapted from	The play is adapted from the Greek.
adapted to	He soon adapted himself to the situation.
agree to	She will undoubtedly agree to the proposal.
agree on	The staff has agreed on the use of the cafeteria.
agree with	The directors agree with the officers on the various benefit plans.
anger at (conditions, animals)	They are angry at the elevator service.
anger with (a person)	She is angry with the telephone operator.
argue about	Do not argue about the shortage of material.

argue for	The group argued for shorter working hours.
argue with	He argued with his friend about the market price.
beside	The girl is standing beside her mother.
besides	Besides benefiting the employees, the plan will also help the consumers.
consist in	Happiness does not always consist in possessing money.
consist of	Synthetics consist of many ingredients.
convenient for	A Tuesday meeting will be convenient for the group.
convenient to	The place of venue was not convenient to the plaintiff.
died from	She died from the debris of the helicopter.
died of	Ray died of malaria in the Far East.
differ about	We differ about the landing of certain airplanes.
differ from	Your car differs from mine in several respects.
differ in	The executives differ in their opinions about expansion.
differ on	They often differ on the question of dividends.
differ with	Mr. Dunn differs with the Personnel Manager on Employment practices.
enter at	The sign directs us to enter at the front gate.
enter for	He placed his bid to enter for the trophy.
enter in	The accountant will enter the transactions in the ledger.

enter into	The partners entered into an agreement to do business abroad.
enter upon	He will soon enter upon a new career.
impatient at	The purchaser was impatient at the delay in delivery.
impatient of	He is impatient of the outcome of his investments.
impatient with	The boss is becoming impatient with his secretary because of her many errors.
inquire at	The visitors inquired at the information desk.
inquire after	Your friend has inquired after (or about) your health.
inquire about	The consignee is inquiring about the shipment.
inquire of	She inquired of the telephone operator regarding long distance rates.
inquire into	I shall inquire into the reasons why he refused to sign the document.

The following illustrations may help in the correct use of some prepositions:

Use *from* with persons; *off* with things:

1. I accepted the gift *from* the donor.
2. He blew the dust *off* the old desk.

Use could *have*; could *of* is incorrect:

I could *have* danced all night.

Do not confuse *behind* with *in back of*:

1. There is a parking lot *behind* the building.
2. The striker is carrying a sign *in back of* him.

Use *as*, not *like*, in certain instances:

1. Do *as* (not *like*) the doctor tells you.
2. I feel *as if* (not *like*) I should take a vacation.

They drove *into* the parking lot.
He is going *in to* see his father in his office.

The decision was based *upon* the facts.
The books were *up on* a high shelf.

She is free *from* (not *of*) any obligation in this matter.
I differ *from* (or *with*) your opinion.
The two partners differ *about* (or *over*) the question of office space.

The boy was unequal *to* (not *for*) the task.

She is *somewhat* (not *some*) better.

Where shall we *go*? (not *go to*)

Native speakers use idiomatic expressions quite naturally and effectively. At times, however, they may have difficulty in choosing the appropriate preposition. It is recommended that a dictionary or word usage book be consulted in case of doubt as to correct usage.

7. Conjunctions

Conjunctions introduce and connect clauses and join series of words and phrases. They fall into three classes: *coordinating*, *correlative* and *subordinating*.

a. Coordinating conjunctions

Coordinating conjunctions are used to connect words or phrases or to connect clauses that are of equal rank. The principal coordinating conjunctions are *and*, *but*, *for*, *nor*, *or*, *yet*.

Tom *or* John will distribute the mail.
(connecting word to word)

On my lunch hour I will go to the bank *and* to the post office.
(connecting phrase to phrase)

I intended to go by plane, *but* I decided to drive my car. (connecting independent clause to independent clause)

I informed him that the order was received *and* that it would be shipped today.
(connecting dependent clause to independent clause)

b. Correlative conjunctions

Correlative conjunctions work in pairs to connect elements of equal grammatical rank. Correlatives must be placed immediately before the combinations they connect. Some of the common correlatives are *not only/but also, neither/nor, either/or, both/and, whether/or.*

The company believes that there should be uniform treatment *not only* of all expenditures, *but also* of deferred tax accounting.

No party to this proceeding, *neither* staff *nor* affected customers, supports the peak load pricing proposal.

The corporation submits that it is inappropriate to recognize *either* an increase in property taxes *or* an increase in operating expenses.

Please advise *whether or* not it will be convenient for you to attend the meeting on Thursday.

c. Subordinating Conjunctions

When one idea in a sentence is dependent upon another, a subordinating conjunction is used to connect the dependent clause with the principal clause. Subordinating conjunctions express relationships such as cause and result, manner or method, condition, contrast, time, place, and purpose. Some common subordinating conjunctions are *after, as soon as, because, if, inasmuch as, more than, since, though, unless, when, while.*

We shall appreciate your effecting the transfer of the stock *as soon as* you can conveniently do so.

If several programs are planned, it may pay to buy or develop a good mailing list.

A contract specifying the terms will be signed *when* an oral agreement is reached.

While recognizing the potential benefits of an examination, some managers feel that the weaknesses of the procedure outweigh the advantages.

The report will be studied at a meeting *after* the salesmen have had an opportunity to study the items included therein.

8. Interjections

An interjection is a part of speech expressing emotion in the form of an exclamation. Mild interjections are set off by commas; strong interjections require an exclamation point.

Oh, well, we can try again tomorrow.

Act now! Vote today!

Man! What a show!

Since the use of interjections is obvious, no detailed discussion is necessary. It should be noted, however, that no comma or period is used after an exclamation point.

"Get out out of the room!" he screamed.

He screamed, "Get out of the room!"

B. PARTS OF SPEECH RELATIVE TO USE IN A SENTENCE

Each word in our language, as a part of speech, is classified according to its function in a sentence as well as by its intrinsic form. A noun may be used as a subject, a modifier, a direct object, or the object of a preposition. The same word may be used as a noun, an adjective, or as a verb (when the accent is changed). For example, the words *present*, *produce*, etc.

pres′/ent	He was happy to receive the *present.*	(noun)
	It is impossible to give you an answer at the *present* time.	(adjective)

pre/sent′	Mr. Jones, may I *present* my husband Jack Singer.	(verb)
prod′/uce	The *produce* of oil reserves is much in demand.	(noun)
pro/duce′	Anything out of the ordinary will *produce* a flood of rumors.	(verb)

1. Content and Structure Words

Words in the English language may be classified as *content* words or *structure* words. *Content* words constitute the majority of words and are called nouns, verbs, adjectives, and adverbs; *structure* words include pronouns, prepositions, conjunctions, and interjections. Structure words provide a framework for organizing content words into meaningful sentences. Some words may be labeled differently as their functions differ. A noun may change its function by adapting to the possessive form:

John is here. (noun)

John's hat is here. (adjective)

An adjective changes to an adverb by the addition of *-ly*:

Evelyn looked *curious. (adjective)*

Mark looked curiously at the package. (adverb)

A word may be classifed as a *verb* or a *noun* according to its use in a sentence:

The boy *was running* down the street. (verb)
Running is good exercise. (gerund = verb form used as a noun)

The word *that* may be used in several ways:

The news is *that* a storm is coming. (conjunction introducing a noun clause)

That desk is sturdy. (adjective)

Additional examples could be cited indicating the various uses of certain words in the English language. The main point here is to illustrate that the part of speech of a word is determined by its use in a sentence.

New words or new definitions of old words frequently enter the *content* class of words, thus expanding the English language. While new *structure* words rarely enter the language, the grammatical behavior of some structure words is complex.

2. Rhetoric in Business Communications

Business communications have to be clear, concise, and to the point. Usually time is of the essence so that there is little opportunity for showiness or elaboration in language or literary style. Rhetoric, however, is important because words have to be used effectively in speaking and in writing so as to influence, persuade, or convince. It is becoming increasingly more important for all businessmen to possess a ready and accurate command of the English language and to be quite skilled in the art and science of literary composition. To this end, a knowledge of correct sentence structure is necessary because the use of an incorrect word or a misplaced modifier can alter the meaning of a sentence. A good vocabulary along with the understanding of the use of words will result in more effective communication.

It is impossible here to analyze and to give detailed rules for agreement of subject with verb, compound words, or collective nouns; the use of adjectives and adverbs; or the proper combinations of content and structure words. Illustrative examples will be limited to words frequently misused in business, misplaced modifiers, or poorly constructed sentences.

Correct: If anyone calls, tell *him* I'll return at four.
Incorrect: If anyone calls, tell them I'll return at four.

Correct: *Who* is calling?
Incorrect: Whom is calling?

Correct: He gave the letters to Doris and *me*.
Incorrect: He gave the letters to Doris and myself.

Correct: Mr. Jones and *I* will attend the meeting.
Incorrect: Mr. Jones and myself will attend the meeting.

Correct:	If you are agreeable to *having* your brother act as executor of your estate, please let me know.
Incorrect:	If you are agreeable to have your brother act as executor of your estate, please let me know.
Correct:	I should *have* read the article.
Incorrect:	I should of read the article.
Correct:	*She* and Joan are working late.
Incorrect:	Her and Joan are working late.
Correct:	It won't do *any* good to tell him.
Incorrect:	It won't do no good to tell him.
Correct:	*We* girls believe we should get new typewriters.
Incorrect:	Us girls believe we should get new typewriters.
Correct:	Coffee is served in the morning for *us* employees.
Incorrect:	Coffee is served in the morning for we employees.
Correct:	*Whose* desk are you using?
Incorrect:	Who's desk are you using?
Correct:	*It's* going to rain.
Incorrect:	Its going to rain.
Correct:	*Economics* is an interesting subject.
Incorrect:	Economics are an interesting subject.
Correct:	Taxes, in addition to interest, *are* included in mortgage payments.
Incorrect:	Taxes in addition to interest is included in mortgage payments.
Correct:	The rest of the travelers *were* housed in inns.
Incorrect:	The rest of the travelers was housed in inns.
Correct:	One of the men *is* dictating the letters.
Incorrect:	One of the men are dictating the letters.
Correct:	Give the message to *whoever* answers the telephone.
Incorrect:	Give the message to whomever answers the telephone.

Correct: The goods *are* on display in the showroom.
Incorrect: The goods is on display in the showroom.

Correct: *Who* shall I say is calling?
Incorrect: Whom shall I say is calling?

Correct: If this *were* true, I would accept your offer.
Incorrect: If this was true, I would accept your offer.

Correct: Tell him to *lie* down for an hour.
Incorrect: Tell him to lay down for an hour.

Correct: I have *lain* in bed all day.
Incorrect: I have laid in bed all day.

Correct: If the enclosed document *be* in order, please sign where indicated.
Incorrect: If the enclosed document is in order, please sign where indicated.

Correct: After working for several hours, *I was still unable to find the error.*
Incorrect: After working for several hours, the error still could not be found.

Correct: In answering the letter, *Mr. Brown said nothing about the problem.*
Incorrect: In answering the letter, nothing was said about the problem.

Correct: Do you object to *his* going to California?
Incorrect: Do you object to him going to California?

Correct: What *kind of car* are you buying?
Incorrect: What kind of a car are you buying?

Correct: What *type of person* is George?
Incorrect: What type of a person is George?

Correct: I didn't see him *anywhere.*
Incorrect: I didn't see him nowhere.

Correct: We *could hardly* see the road because of the fog.
Incorrect: We couldn't hardly see the road because of the fog.

Correct: The milk tastes *sour.*
Incorrect: The milk tastes sourly.

Correct:	The book is *really* interesting.
Incorrect:	The book is real interesting.
Correct:	This is a *newly painted* house.
Incorrect:	This is a newly-painted house.
Correct:	Grace is *somewhat* older than her husband.
Incorrect:	Grace is some older than her husband.
Correct:	I will *try to* meet the deadline.
Incorrect:	I will try and meet the deadline.
Correct:	I am not *unmindful* of you.
Incorrect:	I am not unmindful about you.
Correct:	She is *in search of* a rare antique.
Incorrect:	She is in search for a rare antique.
Correct:	You *will attend either* the morning or afternoon meeting.
Incorrect:	You will either attend the morning or afternoon meeting.
Correct:	Proofreading is a process of reading for errors.
Incorrect:	Proofreading is where you read material for errors.
Correct.	Books, pamphlets, *etc.,* are sold at the corner store.
Incorrect:	Books, pamphlets, and etc. are sold at the corner store.
Correct:	I am doubtful *that* he can complete the work.
Incorrect:	I am doubtful if he can complete the work.
Correct:	*Attached is* my bill for services rendered.
Incorrect:	Attached herewith is my bill for services rendered.
Correct:	They discussed the matter *during* their meeting.
Incorrect:	They discussed the matter in the course of their meeting.
Correct:	Please return the document *when* you have signed it.
Incorrect:	Please return the document if and when you have signed it.

Correct: *She is* frequently in the news.
Incorrect: She is a woman who is frequently in the news.

Correct: *Often* we are unable to find addresses for old stockholders.
Incorrect: Oftentimes we are unable to find addresses for old stockholders.

Correct: The reason for her leaving the firm *is that* she is moving out of town.
Incorrect: The reason for her leaving the firm is because she is moving out of town.

Correct: *Those* people have been waiting on line for one hour.
Incorrect: Them people have been waiting on line for one hour.

Correct: Foods containing grain or wheat are *healthful.*
Incorrect: Foods containing grain or wheat are healthy.

Correct: I differ *with* her on her approach to the matter.
Incorrect: I differ from her on her approach to the matter.

Correct: The child acts *as if* he were happy.
Incorrect: The child acts like he was happy.

SUMMARY

Chapter 2 discusses briefly the eight parts of speech, indicating that the content words, such as nouns, verbs, adjectives, and adverbs constitute the majority of words in the English language, and that new words frequently enter the content class. The structure words such as pronouns, prepositions, conjunctions, and interjections provide a framework for organizing content words into meaningful sentences. Included in the chapter are various types of nouns and pronouns; categories and functions of verbs; similarities and differences between adjectives and adverbs; and the functions of prepositions, conjunctions, and interjections. Illustrative sentences are provided to clarify the correct meaning and usage of words and expressions. The aim of the chapter is to acquaint the secretary with a knowledge of rhetoric—the effective and meaningful use of words and the techniques of correct sentence structure.

Chapter 3

MODERN SOLUTIONS TO PUNCTUATION PROBLEMS

Punctuation is used to clarify the meaning of a sentence, to help the reader understand the thought more readily, and to assist a person who is reading aloud to phrase and emphasize coherently. Most punctuation is placed according to definite rules which apply without exception. There are instances, however, when the rules are arbitrary and punctuation is left to the discretion of the writer.

The secretary must have the ability to punctuate correctly, whether she is transcribing from shorthand notes or from a dictating machine, because executives at times fail to include punctuation when they dictate. A misplaced punctuation mark can change the meaning of a letter, a memorandum or a legal document; an error can result in a cost of thousands of dollars.

A. PUNCTUATION AT THE END OF A SENTENCE

Each sentence ends with a period, an exclamation point, or a question mark.

1. The period

a. A period is used after declarative and imperative sentences, after simple or polite requests, and after an indirect question.

You may take advantage of this special offer only while your present subscription is still in effect. (declarative)

Give me a complete report about the collision. (imperative)

Please send me a loan application. (simple request)

Will you please let us know when you will visit the art exhibit. (polite request)

The president asked me if I would write a memorandum regarding the sale of the cooperative apartment. (indirect question)

The secretary wanted to know if the mail had been delivered. (indirect question)

b. When a period occurs at the same point as a quotation mark or an asterisk, the period usually precedes the quotation mark or the asterisk.

The salesman said, "This is the best buy in town."

We refer to the recent book written by Joe Hart.*

c. The period is also used at the end of some constructions that are not sentences, for example, after abbreviations and initials:

U.S.A. Ph.D. B.C. Dr. Mrs.
Mr. L. D. Flynn f.o.b. N.J. N.H. N.Y.

Exceptions: Abbreviations composed of several capital letters are frequently written without periods:

AAA	American Automobile Association
EDT	Eastern Daylight Time
FM	Frequency Modulation

The new two-letter state abbreviations:

NJ	New Jersey	CA	California	
NH	New Hampshire	IA	Iowa	etc.
NY	New York			

Note: Use of the period is further discussed in connection with other abbreviations, numerals, ellipsis marks, etc.

2. The Exclamation Point

a. An exclamation point is used after a word, a phrase, or a sentence to indicate strong emotion or emphasis.

Congratulations! You won the award for the best suggestion! Come to the stage immediately!

b. An exclamation point is used at the end of a sentence, interrogatory in form, but exclamatory in meaning.

What opportunities are available for young accountants who work diligently!

c. When an exclamation is neither emotional nor emphatic, use a comma instead of the exclamation point.

"So that's what you're planning," said Ruth.

d. The exclamation is often used to express irony or surprise.

She claimed the necklace contained real(!) alexandrite stones.

Surprise! Happy Birthday!

3. The Question Mark

a. The question mark is used after a direct question that calls for an answer in *words*.

Where are you going on your vacation?

b. If the request is stated in question form, but the answer calls for *action* rather than words, a period is used.

Will you please review the pension plan and let us have your comments.

May we suggest that you notify the bank immediately concerning your lost checkbook.

c. Use the question mark after a question which occurs within a sentence.

As a graduate of the City—or is it the State University?—she has achieved success in a short time.

d. If a sentence contains a clause questioning the entire sentence, set off the clause with commas, and use a question mark at the end of the sentence.

You had a chance, didn't you, to win the race?

e. Use a question mark to express more than one question in the same sentence.

Do you consider her loyal? trustworthy? intelligent? dependable?

f. A question mark is sometimes used to indicate doubt.

The new houses are selling for $80,000(?) at the present time.

B. INTERNAL PUNCTUATION

1. The Comma

The most commonly used mark of punctuation, aside from end punctuation, is the comma, which presents more problems than any other mark of punctuation. A comma is used or not used according to sentence structure and meaning. There are certain basic rules for the use of the comma, and there are also exceptions to the rules.

a. Comma in a Series

The most controversial use of the comma is whether or not to use a comma before "and" in a series. While the rule states that a comma is used to separate three or more items in a series, the use of a comma before "and" depends on the form and meaning of the sentence.

(1) Commas separate words and phrases in a series:

> The dress illustrated in the catalog is available in red, brown, black, and white.
> [The comma before *and* is necessary for clarification. If the comma were omitted, the reader might infer that the color was a mixture of black and white.]
>
> By his decisions in the market place, the consumer tells the manufacturer what he prefers, what he will buy, and the price he is willing to pay.

If there is no danger of misreading, the comma may be omitted before *and* in a series.

> For breakfast this morning, I had coffee, toast, ham and eggs.
>
> Please order paper, pencils, erasers and notebooks.

(2) Use a comma between coordinate adjectives not linked by a coordinating conjunction:

> It is a humid, dreary, rainy day.

(3) If two constituents in a series are not joined by a coordinating conjunction, they are separated by a comma.

> He can afford to live without working, to spend money without reckoning.

b. Comma Between Coordinate Adjectives

Coordinate adjectives are adjectives of equal rank that precede a noun. Use a comma to separate two or more coordinate adjectives.

They were on a long, enjoyable boat ride.
He is a young, inexperienced worker.

[Coordinate adjectives can be reversed in order, separated by *and*, or used individually as predicate adjectives.]

Do not use a comma when the adjectives are not coordinate:

She is a competent social worker.

[There is no comma because the adjectives are not coordinate, or of equal importance; *social* modifies worker; competent modifies *social worker.* The adjectives could not be reversed to read: She is a social competent worker.]

c. Comma with Independent and Dependent Clauses

(1) Independent Clauses

A comma is used to separate independent clauses that are joined by one of the following coordinate conjunctions: *and, but, for, nor, or.*

They intended to complete the work on Wednesday, but they could not go to the office because of the blackout.

No comma is required in a short clause:

You go your way and I'll go mine.

If two independent clauses are contrasted in meaning, a comma is necessary:

That is a good offer, but I believe I can do better.

A comma is not necessary with a compound predicate:

We are not required to answer the questions but are delighted to do so.

If a subject is understood in each independent clause, as in an imperative sentence, a comma is recommended:

Go to the post office, and have this letter sent by registered mail.

(2) *Dependent Clauses*

When a dependent clause precedes an independent clause, set it off with a comma. Dependent clauses begin with such words as *although, because, if, that, unless, when,* etc.

If you wish further information, please telephone me.

Do not place a comma after a dependent clause that is the subject of a sentence:

Where they will go now is the question.

(a) *Nonrestrictive Elements*

Nonrestrictive means that an element can be taken out of the sentence without affecting the meaning or identity of the object it describes. While most nonrestrictive modifiers are used as adjectives, nonrestrictive elements can also be infinitive or participial phrases, or occasionally an adverbial clause. Nonrestrictive elements are set off by commas.

Such an increment, which is obviously an incentive to management, in the end result will also benefit the ratepayer.
(nonrestrictive adjective clause)

The decision of the company's management, implementing income tax provisions, will be taken into consideration.
(nonrestrictive participial phrase)

Last year the Company sold 500,000 shares of its common stock, as you know.
(nonrestrictive adverb clause in its natural order)

Mr. Paul Fritz, who will be out of town in December, will be unable to attend the annual meeting.
(nonrestrictive adjective clause)

(b) *Essential Subordinate Clause*

Do not use commas to set off a subordinate clause that occurs within or follows an independent clause if it is essential to the meaning of a sentence.

The young boy who won the tennis match had played tennis for several years.

d. Clauses and Phrases Out of Their Natural Order

When adverbial clauses or infinitive and participial phrases introduce a sentence, they should be followed by a comma.

When Mr. Goodward returns to his office, ask him to call me.
(adverb clause at beginning of sentence)

Standing unnoticed at the party, Mr. Hale could observe the other guests.
(participial phrase at beginning of sentence)

To watch the parade, we had to go to the front of the building.
(infinitive phrase at beginning of sentence)

e. Appositive Elements

An appositive may be removed from a sentence without destroying the meaning of the sentence. Appositives are words, phrases, or clauses, and should be set off from the rest of the sentence by the use of commas. One-word appositives are not set off by commas.

Mr. Frank Hayde, *the President of our Corporation,* is on a business trip to the Far East.

Two of our salesmen, *Mr. Clarke and Mr. Townsend,* will attend the meeting in St. Louis, Missouri.

My brother *Bernard* is studying law. (one-word appositive)

f. Parenthetical Expressions

Parenthetical words or phrases depart from the main thought of the sentence. These elements may contrast, explain, amend, or qualify some part of the sentence, but they are not grammatically necessary to the sentence. Some of the frequently used words and phrases are: *as you know, finally, however, in fact, nevetheless, of course, therefore,* etc. When these expressions join two clauses, a semicolon usually precedes them.

We were not, *as you know,* aware of the problem; *consequently* Gordon will be afforded relief whenever such is necessary, as is the present request.

The rate proposed by the staff is close to the competitive price; *therefore,* the Company urges that the rate be tied to the recommended price of oil.

Note: Commas may be omitted from parenthetical expressions to avoid overpunctuation and when such expressions do not interrupt the thought or obscure the meaning of a sentence.

You will of course accept the offer.

We are accordingly signing the agreement.

Moreover it is too late to withdraw from the plan.

The price is acceptable. I will therefore send you a check as soon as I receive your invoice.

g. Direct Address

Use a comma to set off persons or objects that are addressed in speaking or writing.

Mr. Egan, your portfolio is in my office. We trust, Mr. Mann, that you will understand our position.

Ronald, please make four copies of this letter.

h. Explanatory or Identifying Elements

Use commas to set off explanatory or identifying elements that are not essential to the meaning of the sentence.

Innate differences in abilities serve to restrict the number of high-paid managers, in particular, and limit the number of persons available.

The plans for the new office, including facilities for the staff, were approved.

Tuesday, June 30, is the deadline for submitting the bid.

Denver, Colorado, is my birthplace.

Mr. Dwayne Carr, of Larchmont, Connecticut, addressed the meeting.

Note: When only a month and year are given, no punctuation is necessary.

When a person's name is set off in solid capitals, as in a Will, no commas are necessary.

I bequeath to my son JAMES MARTIN one-third of my residuary estate.

When the title of a book or magazine is set off in solid capitals, no commas are necessary.

A copy of the useful book ZIP CODE DIRECTORY should be available in every office.

The June 1929 issue of THE WORLD is not available in the local library.

Do not use commas when the explaining or identifying words are essential to the meaning of the sentence.

The word *excellent* is frequently misspelled.

The author Irwin Shaw was born in 1913.

The schedule to be proofread is on Mr. Baker's desk.

i. Inverted Names, Two Numbers Coming Together, and Repeated Words

A comma is necessary when listing names in inverted order, when two numbers run together, and when the same word is repeated. The order of words in a sentence can sometimes be changed to avoid using the comma.

> Please type a list of employees, placing the last name first; for example, Mitchell, Frances M.
>
> In 1977, 5,000 stores were looted in a blackout in New York City.
>
> In 1977, at the time of the blackout in New York City, 5,000 stores were looted.
>
> Run, run as fast as you can!
>
> Whatever you do, do it well.

j. Numbers Written With and Without Commas

A comma is used in numbers of four or more digits. A comma is not used in writing years, policy numbers, page numbers, telephone numbers, addresses, and decimals.

$2,500,000	the year 1980
1,110 kilometers	page 1156
4,500 pounds	13651 Charlevoix Drive
Policy #60056743-57	(201) 465-7500

> In the metric system, one kilometer is equal to 3280.8 feet or 0.621 mile.

k. Introductory or Transitional Words and Phrases

(1) Use a comma after a long introductory prepositional phrase. No comma is needed if the prepositional phrase is short.

> At the suggestion of Mr. Ralph Rowe, I am writing to you for information concerning your new sailboats.
>
> Within a month you will have details of our merger.

(2) Use a comma after an introductory phrase that contains a verb form.

> Upon motion duly made and seconded, the reading of the minutes of the previous meeting was waived.

To cancel the indebtedness, the debtor was forced to surrender his stock.

(3) Use a comma after a transitional or introductory word that is not essential to the basic meaning of a sentence.

Generally speaking, the decision was just and equitable.

Note: Short introductory prepositional phrases need not be followed by a comma.

In summer 1976 a violent storm hit Fire Island.

During the past five years the corporation's profits steadily increased.

l. To Show Omission of Words

Use a comma to indicate the omission of a word, usually a word that has already been used in the sentence.

Jones prefers to invest in stocks; Smith, in bonds; and Williams, in mortgages.

The comma is omitted, however, if the meaning is clear without it.

Nancy's chief interest is music; John's is sports; and Robert's is riding horseback.

m. The Comma Used for Clarity

Occasionally a comma may be needed for clarification and to prevent misreading, although it is not prescribed by a specific rule.

Those who can, do; those who cannot, teach.

A few days before, I met her in California.

Please come in, in a few weeks.

n. Misused Commas

Commas should not be used unnecessarily in a sentence, nor should they obstruct meaning. A comma should not separate a subject from the verb; a verb from its complement, direct object, or modifiers.

> The candidate I favor, is the one who is for the people, not for the politicians.
> (the comma after "favor" should be omitted)
>
> That I was surprised, was apparent.
> (omit comma)
>
> The cause of the accident was, that the driver went through a red light.
> (omit comma)

A comma is not used between adjectives that are not coordinate; that is, when adjectives are not of the same rank, or when they are too closely related to be separated.

> He looked at the report with his narrow squinty eyes.

A comma is not used when the conjunction connects all words in a series.

> He is the smartest and wittiest and best man in the office.

Do not separate compound personal pronouns from the words they emphasize.

> She herself mailed the letter.

Omit periods and commas when II, III, or IV are used with names.

Henry IV
William Lee III
John Abbott II

Note: A comma may or may not be used before or after Jr. and Sr. in a name; Inc. or Ltd. in a company name.

Barry Grant, Jr. *or* Barry Grant Jr.
Dunbar Inc. *or* Dunbar, Inc.
Lefko, Ltd. *or* Lefko Ltd.

2. The Semicolon

The semicolon calls for a pause as long as a period, but it is used only as internal punctuation. A trend in modern writing is to make less frequent use of the semicolon. Periods and semicolons are sometimes interchangeable.

a. A semicolon is used to separate two independent clauses in a compound sentence when the conjunction is omitted or when the connection is not close.

A wise man thinks and then acts; an impetuous man acts and then thinks.

b. A semicolon is used to separate two independent clauses joined by a connective other than a coordinate conjunction.

The President was unavoidably detained; nevertheless, the meeting proceeded as scheduled, with Mr. James Moran acting as Chairman.

In a large law office there are several divisions; for example, specific areas are corporate, tax, estates, real estate, and litigation.

The client was thoroughly satisfied with the provisions of the Will; therefore he signed it immediately before two witnesses.

Note: The comma after the conjunctive adverb is a matter of choice; at times it is not necessary because of the flow of thought. Some authorities use it; others do not.

c. A semicolon is placed outside quotation marks.

At the December meeting, President Moore said, "I do not wish to continue in office"; however, we hope he will change his mind.

d. A semicolon is placed after parentheses when the parenthetical matter is used to explain the preceding item.

> In proofreading, a correction should be made in the margin on the same line as the error. If there is more than one error in a particular line, the corrections should appear in order, separated by a slant line (e.g., l.c./tr/stet); both margins may be used for [proofreader's] marks.

e. Use a semicolon before conjunctive adverbs that join two independent clauses when the clauses are long or when they contain commas.

> Traditional lawsuits involved sharply defined factual issues; conversely, legal controversies today focus on social issues on which data are never conclusive.

> From information in our files, we can formulate appropriate answers to the interrogatories; however, if you believe there is anything out of the ordinary, please advise us.

f. Use a semicolon to separate the items in a series when one or more of the items contains a comma, and when the list of items would not be clear if separated by commas.

> The survey was made in Cheyenne, Wyoming, and Salem, Oregon; and the results were analyzed in San Francisco, California, and Phoenix, Arizona.

3. The Colon

The colon is used to introduce a list, enumerations, statements, or illustrations. A colon usually appears after the words *as follows* and *following*.

a. A colon introduces listed items.

> The employment contract provides that the employee may not disclose confidential information relating to the following: practices, procedures, processes, formulas, compounds, production costs, or customer relations of the company.

In preparing any type of writing, the following format is necessary:

1. Beginning
2. Middle
3. Ending

b. A colon introduces a formal or long direct quotation.

The Corporation hereby adopts the following amendment to the Employee's Retirement Plan:

"Normal Retirement Date means the 65th anniversary of the Employee's date of birth or the 10th anniversary of the year in which the Employee commenced participation in the Plan, whichever is later."

c. A colon follows a formal salutation in a letter.

Dear sir:
Gentlemen:
Dear Ms. Grant:

d. A colon is used in the following special instances:

(1) Between figures denoting hours, minutes, seconds.

Some employees in our office work from 8:30 to 4:30; others work from 9:30 to 5:30.

(2) To separate chapter and verse.

The following quotation appears in James 3:18.

"And the fruit of justice is sown in peace, to them that make peace."

(3) To express ratios.

The vote was 9:5 in favor of the resolution.

Marks of punctuation such as the period, commas, semicolons and colons are used to clarify the meaning of a sentence.

The test rule for the comma in particular is this: If it makes the meaning clearer, put it in; if not, leave it out. The meanings of the following sentences change with the punctuation:

What do you think I want? Your money?

What! Do you think I want your money?

What do you think? I want your money.

Incorrect: The current was strong, he could not swim. (comma splice)

Incorrect: The current was strong he could not swim. (run-on sentence)

Correct: The current was so strong that he could not swim.

Correct: Because the current was strong, he could not swim.

C. QUOTATION MARKS

Quotation marks are used to set off direct quotations, certain titles, and words used in a specific manner. Other marks of punctuation are placed in proper relation to quotation marks; for example, explanatory words and the speaker are placed outside quotation marks or are enclosed in brackets within the quotation.

1. Direct Quotation

The foreman stated: "The drainage structure under the building [with its connecting pipe to other structures] is part of a drainage network."

When a direct quotation is used within a direct quotation, the internal quotation is enclosed in single quotation marks and the entire question in regular quotation marks:

The Trust Agreement reads: "The Trustee may pay all or any part of the principal to the 'person' acting as 'guardian' for the minor."

An indirect quotation is not enclosed by quotation marks:

The defendant's answer stated that the plaintiff should enumerate the dates on which each event occurred.

Explanatory expressions are placed outside quotation marks, and can appear before, within, or at the end of the quotation. Short explanatory material is usually set off from the direct quotation by commas; lengthy explanatory material is set off by a colon.

It was John F. Kennedy, 35th President of the United States, who said: "The human mind is our fundamental resource."

"In distributive education," the director said, "work experience is provided for students in stores and offices in the community."

2. Quoted Material

When quotations consist of more than one paragraph, quotation marks are placed at the beginning of each paragraph and at the end of the last paragraph.

The proposal stated:

"It should be pointed out that if the agreements between the Company and Central Electric are approved, the gas turbines will be used as originally anticipated.

"The Company recognizes that fluctuations will occur in maintenance costs and therefore does not object to the use of a five-year average to determine a normal level of maintenance expense."

Except in legal work, when words and punctuation marks must be copied exactly as written, the following rules pertain with regard to the use of quotation marks:

Quotation marks are always placed *OUTSIDE* the comma and the period. They are placed *OUTSIDE* the quotation mark and exclamation point when only the quoted part denotes a question or an exclamation. For example:

> Helen asked, "Are you leaving now?"
>
> The office boy screamed "Fire!"

Quotation marks are placed *OUTSIDE* the dash, when it stands for something unsaid:

> The testimony read: "On cross-examination, the witness agreed—among other things—"

Quotation marks are placed *OUTSIDE* the parenthesis, when the entire parenthetical clause is quoted; for example,

> The testimony stated: "The slope on the retention basin is no greater than the slope on a normal highway bridge approach (Tr. 17, 4-5)" and further . . .

Quotation marks are placed *INSIDE* the colon and semicolon:

> The following monies are due and owing under the "Collateral Agreement": interest in the amount of $450; costs and disbursements in the sum of $75.
>
> With a cooperative, the tenant-owner receives a "proprietary lease"; in a condominium, the purchaser actually owns a specific apartment.

Quotation marks are placed INSIDE the question mark and exclamation point when the entire sentence is a question or an exclamation:

> Did I hear him say, "I can't go today"?
>
> The speaker exclaimed, "What irony"!

Quotation marks are placed *INSIDE* the dash, when it is used as an ordinary punctuation mark.

> Lewis Carroll's Humpty Dumpty said: "When I use a word, it means just what I choose it to mean—neither more nor less. . . . The question is . . . which is to be master"—

Quotation marks are placed *INSIDE* the parentheses when the parenthetical clause alone is quoted:

> Noel Coward's famous quote ("Mad dogs and Englishmen go out in the mid-day sun") is good advice to sun-lovers.
>
> *Note:* Explanatory material, when brief, is set off from the direct quotation by a comma; when explanatory material is lengthy, a colon precedes the direct quotation.

3. Ellipses

Ellipses signify omissions in quotations, hesitation in narrative or dialogue, or they separate statements in advertising material. Three periods indicate an omission of words within or at the beginning of a sentence. When the omission of words occurs at the end of a sentence, a fourth period is used in addition to the three periods. Three stars (* * *) are also used to indicate an ellipsis in the body of a paragraph or at the end.

> "We contribute little individually," Aristotle writes . . . but, he adds, "by the united effort of all a considerable amount. . . ."
>
> *Note.* In typing ellipses, space once after the word; then alternate periods and spaces. At the end of a sentence, the period is placed immediately after the word, followed by alternate spaces and periods.

D. BREAKS WITHIN A SENTENCE

Dashes, parentheses, and brackets indicate breaks within a sentence and are used to denote nonessential elements, a change of thought, explanatory words, or emphasis.

1. Dash

a. The *dash* is used to set off a comment that is long or that is a complete sentence in itself.

Term insurance means exactly what the name implies—coverage for a certain length of time, which you specify.

b. The *dash* is used to set off a nonessential constituent that contains commas of its own.

Vocational subjects—accounting, data processing, shorthand, and typewriting—are experiencing increasing enrollments.

c. The *dash* is used to indicate an abrupt change in a sentence.

In a dog—just as in a chimpanzee—the brainpan is smaller and the jaws are larger than in man.

d. The *dash* is used to set off explanatory matter.

If a person renews an insurance policy—a transaction known as renewable term insurance, available without another medical examination—the cost rises because the policy holder is now older.

e. The *dash* is used to indicate an unfinished sentence.

Before you sign your name, read—

Note: In typing, use two hyphens to make a dash. Some writers prefer to leave a space before and after the dash; other writers leave no spaces before or after the dash. In either case, the writer must be consistent.

2. Parentheses (ses = plural; parenthes*is* = singular)

a. *Parentheses* are used to enclose nonessential, explanatory, or isolated material.

Study has helped some people obtain better jobs or make more money. (Other people simply value their new knowledge and derive satisfaction from it.)

Whatever type of appliance you purchase, be sure to get (and read) your warranty.

b. *Parentheses* are used to enclose letters or figures marking divisions of a topic.

Business letters are governed by three C's: (1) Clarity, (2) Correctness, and (3) Conciseness.

Following are some famous New York restaurants and the characteristic year for each: Fraunces Tavern (1783), Luchow's (1885), Delmonico's (1902), Jack and Charlie's "21" (1929), the Rainbow Room (1934), and Windows of the World (1977).

c. *Parentheses* are used to repeat numbers in legal documents.

On signing of the contract, Purchaser will pay to Seller the sum of Ten Thousand ($10,000) Dollars, representing Ten (10%) Percent of the purchase price.

d. *Parentheses* are used to enclose cross references.

Nursing homes (sometimes called convalescent homes) provide nursing care and related health services to their residents.

In automatic action washers (also called "semiautomatic") each operation is manually started.

Note: If an entire sentence is enclosed in parentheses (following a mark of end punctuation), the period goes inside the final parenthesis. If only a terminal part of a sentence is enclosed in parentheses, the period closing the entire sentence goes outside the parenthesis.

3. Brackets

Square brackets are used to enclose nonquoted material or comments inserted into a quotation.

> The corporation's revenues must be increased to allow the corporation to [actually] earn a higher return on equity.
>
> Aunt Lizzie bequeathed $50,000 to her favorite neice [sic] Helene.
>
> *Note:* A bracketed [sic] denotes that the error appears in the original.

Although brackets are not commonly used in business correspondence, they are used in reports and in legal documents.

E. ITALICS

In handwritten or typewritten papers, italics are indicated by underlining words and phrases, along with the punctuation.

1. *Titles* of books, newspapers, magazines, plays, musical works, movies, and long poems are underlined.

> Ernest Hemingway's <u>The Old Man and the Sea</u> is a gripping story of a fisherman who makes a big catch.
>
> <u>CUE</u> magazine is a popular guide to restaurants and entertainment.
>
> Shakespeare's comedy <u>Midsummer Night's Dream</u> is always a delightful play.
>
> The Rodgers and Hammerstein musical classic <u>The King and I</u> has been revived again and again.
>
> <u>A Streetcar Named Desire,</u> a drama by Tennessee Williams, is a powerful film, magnificent in direction, photography, and performance.
>
> A poem written in Asia by Ch'en Tzu-ang (656-98) and translated by Arthur Waley, entitled <u>Business Men,</u> is philosophical.

2. Italics are used to indicate *foreign* words, but not words that have been Anglicized.

The decision was that the situation was a case of caveat emptor.

The sine qua non of philosopy is the study of principles underlying knowledge.

The raison d'être of business is to make a profit and to be of service to people.

This Court has jurisdiction of this case pursuant to 28 U.S.C. Section 1362, supra.

Karate is a popular subject at present.

3. Use italics for *emphasis*.

Do not leave your door unlocked.
Investigate before you invest.
How much is your time worth?

4. *Legal* usage places in italics the names of plaintiff and defendant in the citation of cases at law.

An employer may discharge an employee on the following grounds: negligence, neglect of duty, and inefficiency. Crane v. Glen Film Company, ibid.

Jurisdiction of the Court is not defeated In re Sumner.

In Ex parte 87, the Court issued a Preliminary Injunction enjoining the State from enforcing its statutes concerning cigarettes.

F. THE APOSTROPHE

1. The apostrophe is used to indicate *possession* and the *omission* of letters.

This is the girl's sweater.

The Imperial Group is a girls' club.

The B'way Businessmen's Ass'n meets on the 15th of each month.

Cornucopia is my brother-in-law's shop.

The singular and plural possessive forms of some nouns sound alike. The context of the sentence, of course, will indicate which form is intended.

The secretary should follow the boss's suggestions.

The entire office should comply with the executive bosses' regulations.

2. The apostrophe is used to form the possessive of *indefinite pronouns*, such as *one*, *everybody*, *everyone*, etc.

Each one's plan for the meeting was in accordance with the theme of the convention.

Everybody's aim in life is to be happy and successful.

3. An apostrophe is *not* used with the possessive form of *personal pronouns: hers*, *his*, *its*, *ours*, *theirs*, *yours*, etc.

The pen is hers; the book, his; and the money, yours.

Note: As in the preceding sentence, a comma may be substituted for a verb in succeeding clauses of parallel construction within a sentence.

4. An apostrophe is used with the last name only to indicate *joint ownership*. The apostrophe is used with both nouns to indicate *separate ownership*.

Grant & Fitch's sporting goods are of high quality.

John and Leo's boat will enter the race.

Helen's and Mary's dogs were winners in the contest.

5. The apostrophe is used to show the possessive case of a noun followed by a *gerund* (the *ing* form of a verb).

Ralph's checking all orders proved fruitful.

6. The apostrophe is used in expressions of *time, value, and measurement:*

You may terminate this lease upon thirty days' notice.
Each buyer was permitted to purchase a dollar's worth.
The world's largest department store is in Chicago.

7. The apostrophe is used in *contractions:*

can't (cannot)	didn't (did not)
it's (it is)	won't (will not)
Class of '70 (1970)	

8. In current usage, the apostrophe is frequently omitted in *organization names:*

Travelers Club
Citizens National Bank
Business Teachers Association

9. The apostrophe is used in the possessive form of a *singular or plural name:*

Harry's Hardware Store
The Children's Bazaar

10. The apostrophe is used in the possessive form of a *singular or plural abbreviation:*

Robert Maier, Sr.'s office
Coleman Bros.' January sale

11. The apostrophe is used to form the possessive of *proper names ending in s:*

a. Possessive form of *singular* proper name of *one syllable:*

James's Charles's

b. Possessive form of *singular* proper name of *more than one syllable:*

Williams' Harris'

c. Possessive form of *plural proper name* ending in s:

The Adamses' house
The Joneses' dog

12. The apostrophe may or may not be used in the plural form of figures, letters, and symbols:

There are four 9's (or 9s) in his telephone number.

The yea's (or yeas) have it.

The do's are positive; the don'ts, negative.

Note: When a word already contains an apostrophe, use only an *s* to form the plural.

The CPA's (or CPAs) looked forward to the 1980's (or 1980s).

Use the #'s (or #s) and %'s (or %s) as symbols.

G. THE ASTERISK

An asterisk is used as a *reference* mark or to indicate *omission*:

The magazine AVENUE* is unique, timely, and interesting.

---

*Avenue Magazine, Inc., New York, N. Y. 10022

When a punctuation mark occurs at the same point as an asterisk, the asterisk follows the punctuation mark:

In the article by Demarest,*
. . . at that time.*

Asterisks are frequently used instead of ellipses, particularly to indicate the omission of one or more paragraphs. They may be separated by one or more spaces:

* * *
*   *   *

H. THE AMPERSAND

Legally, the name of a company should be typed exactly as it appears on a letterhead:

Miller & Co., Inc.
Jefferson & Co. Inc.

I. THE DIAGONAL

The diagonal is used with abbreviations, symbols, and certain fractions:

B/L   c/o   2/10, n/30 $5/M

The president and/or treasurer may sign the checks.

A diagonal is used to construct fractions that are not on the typewriter keyboard. A space (*not* a hyphen) is used between whole numbers and fractions:

8 3/4   15 7/8   (*Not:* 8-3/4   15-7/8)

Do not put keyboard fractions and made fractions in the same sentence:

He wears size 6 1/2 or 6 3/4.
(*not:* He wears size 6½ or 6 3/4.)

J. THE HYPHEN

1. Compound Adjectives

A compound adjective consists of two or more descriptive words serving as a single modifier. A compound adjective is hyphenated when it precedes the noun it modifies:

Rates for first-class mail increased to 15 cents in May 1978.

Up-to-date books are reviewed in the Sunday newspaper.

Ernest Hemingway is a well-known author.

2. Numbers

a. Series of numbers

The hyphen is substituted for the word "through" to indicate a continuous series of numbers:

pp. 105-124 1981-85

b. Compound numbers

(1) A hyphen is used to join words representing compound numbers from 21 to 99:

forty-four one hundred ninety-nine

(2) Hyphenate a fraction when it is used as an adjective:

one-half inch one-fourth piece

c. Double compounds

Hyphenate double compounds having a common base:

two-, three-, and four-hour sessions

long- and short-term loans

d. Compound adjectives and numerals

A hyphen is used when numerals precede other words to form compound adjectives:

60-story building

5-cylinder Diesel engine

five-year-old boy

10-day trial period (10 days' trial)

3. Locations

A hyphen is sometimes used between words denoting locations:

South-Western Business Association

Tri-State Publishing Company

4. Prefixes

The hyphen is used in compounds made up of prefixes to proper names:

anti-Christian	non-European
mid-Atlantic	pseudo-Gothic
neo-Platonism	un-American

Note: A hyphen is not used between a prefix and a word that is not a proper noun:

antisocial	nonessential
bicentennial	semiyearly
coauthor	supermarket

Note: *Hyphenation* is fully discussed in Chapter 6.

SUMMARY

Chapter 3 contains functional principles of punctuation followed by realistic illustrations. It discusses the uses of punctuation at the end of a sentence by means of the period, exclamation point, and question mark. It explains in detail the techniques of internal punctuation through the use of the comma, semicolon, and colon. Other facets of punctuation are also discussed, such as: quotation marks; breaks within a sentence using the dash, parentheses, and brackets; and the use of italics and underscoring to emphasize titles and foreign words. This chapter illustrates various uses of the apostrophe to indicate possession and omission of letters. It also includes techniques for using the asterisk, ampersand, diagonal, and hyphen.

Chapter 4

CURRENT USAGE OF ABBREVIATIONS AND SYMBOLS

An abbreviation is a shortened form of a word or phrase frequently used in technical and legal work, statistical data, and footnotes. Some abbreviations call for periods; others do not (for example: "ad"). Abbreviations should not be confused with contractions. In a contraction, an apostrophe is inserted at the exact point where letters are omitted, and no period follows the contraction. If there is a choice between an abbreviation and a contraction, the abbreviation should be chosen as it not only looks better, but it is also easier to type. For example: secy. (not sec'y); dept. (not dep't); mfg. (not m'f'g). Abbreviations should not be used if there is a possibility that they may be misunderstood. In business letters it is preferable to spell out words rather than to use abbreviations. The keynote in writing is *consistency*. Do not abbreviate in one place and spell out in another.

A. TITLES

1. In sentences where only the surname is used, spell out all titles except Mr., Mrs., Ms., Messrs., and Dr.

Professor and Mrs. Gray met Dr. and Mrs. Buck in Europe.

2. Generally accepted abbreviations are those for academic degrees and those referring to organizations and agencies. Academic degrees require a period after each element, but no internal space:

B.A. Ph.D. Ed.D. LL.B. Litt.D. D.D.S. J.D. *but* C.P.A. or CPA

3. The abbreviations Rev. and Hon. should not be used when preceded by *The*:

The Honorable Joseph P. Martin
Rev. Robert M. Moore

B. PUBLISHED MATERIALS

The name of a magazine or newspaper is stated, followed by the volume number, then in parentheses the date of the issue, and lastly the pages covered by the article:

Geier, Charlotte. "Project In/Vest: Insurance Simulation Insures Learning." *Business Education Forum,* Vol. 32, No. 5 (February, 1978), 15-19.

In legal work, a case citation should indicate what court decided the case, either in the name of the report or in parentheses with the date:

Escott v. BarChris, 283 F. Supp. 2d 643 (1968)

United States of America v. State of Washington, U.S.D.C. (E.D. Wash.) Civil No. 3909

The following foreign expressions are commonly used in all types of publications. Periods are used only with the abbreviations:

e.g. (*exempli gratia,* "for example")
et al. (*et alii,* "and other people")

etc. (*et cetera,* "and other things", "and so forth")
ibid. (*ibidem,* "in the same place")
i.e. (*id est,* "that is")
loc. cit. (*loco citato,* "in the place cited")
N.B. (*nota bene,* "note well")
op. cit. (*opere citato,* "in the work cited")
R.S.V.P., r.s.v.p. (*répondez s'il vous plait*, "please reply")

but:

ad hoc ("for a particular purpose")
idem ("the same")
re or in re ("in the matter of," "concerning")

C. NAMES

1. Persons

In addressing persons, it is acceptable to use with the title and surname:

two initials—Mr. B. L. Macon
given name—Bernard Wolf, Esq.
given name with initial—Francis X. Cleary, M.D.
do *not* use *one* initial—Mrs. M. Walsh

2. Companies

Names of business organizations, unions, societies, and associations often appear in abbreviated forms. When these abbreviations consist of all-capital initials, they may be typed with or without periods, but there is usually no space between the letters. Following is a list of some frequently used abbreviations:

a/c or A/C	account
AFL-CIO	American Federation of Labor and Congress of Industrial Organizations

ASCAP	American Society of Composers, Authors and Publishers
COBOL	Common Business Oriented Language—computer language used in business data processing to prepare a program
CPA or C.P.A.	Certified Public Accountant
ERISA	Employee Retirement Income Security Act (1974)
HP, hp	high pressure
H.P., h.p.	horse power
ICC	Interstate Commerce Commission
Messrs.	Messieurs; plural of Mr.
n.b., N.B.	(Latin: *note bene*) note well
ob.	(latin: *obiit*) he or she died
PR	Public Relations
P.S., p.s.	postscript; P.P.S., p.p.s., additional postscripts
R.N., RN	Registered Nurse
SEC, S.E.C.	Securities and Exchange Commission
TELEX	Automatic teletypewriter exchange service
UHF, U.H.F., uhf, u.h.f.	ultra-high frequency
UN	United Nations

Note: Dictionaries list capitalized abbreviations, along with options if usage is divided. A recent dictionary listed a trademark as (Band-Aid, bandaid).

3. Locations

In business letter writing it is preferable to write out such words as Street, Avenue, or Place; North, South, East, and West are spelled out. Abbreviations are used to indicate sections of a city: NE, NW, SE, SW (or N.E., N.W., S.E., S.W.). The names of cities should not be abbreviated. Long names for cities may be abbreviated for use on addressing equipment, but only in accordance with the regulations of the United States Post Office Department in Washington.

4. Geographic

Geographic names made up of single initials require a period after each initial, but no space after each internal period:

U.S.A. B.W.I. U.S.S.R.

When the geographical abbreviation contains more than single initials, space once after each internal period:

N. Mex. W. Va. S. Dak. Dist. of Col.

The Post Office Department in Washington, D.C. has authorized the following two-letter state abbreviations for use in conjunction with ZIP (Zone Improvement Program) Codes:

Alabama	AL	Montana	MT
Alaska	AK	Nebraska	NE
Arizona	AZ	Nevada	NV
Arkansas	AR	New Hampshire	NH
California	CA	New Jersey	NJ
Colorado	CO	New Mexico	NM
Connecticut	CT	New York	NY
Delaware	DE	North Carolina	NC
District of Columbia	DC	North Dakota	ND
Florida	FL	Ohio	OH
Georgia	GA	Oklahoma	OK
Guam	GU	Oregon	OR
Hawaii	HI	Pennsylvania	PA
Idaho	ID	Puerto Rico	PR
Illinois	IL	Rhode Island	RI
Indiana	IN	South Carolina	SC
Iowa	IA	South Dakota	SD
Kansas	KS	Tennessee	TN
Kentucky	KY	Texas	TX
Louisiana	LA	Utah	UT
Maine	ME	Vermont	VT
Maryland	MD	Virginia	VA
Massachusetts	MA	Virgin Islands	VI
Michigan	MI	Washington	WA
Minnesota	MN	West Virginia	WV
Mississippi	MS	Wisconsin	WI
Missouri	MO	Wyoming	WY

As a result of consultation between Canadian and United States postal authorities, there are standard abbreviations for Canadian Provinces; but these abbreviations are intended for use only where there are space limitations, as in computer addressing equipment:

Alberta	Alta.	AB	Nova Scotia	N.S.	NS
British Columbia	B.C.	BC	Ontario	Ont.	ON
Labrador	Lab.	LB	Prince Edward Island	P.E.I.	PE
Manitoba	Man.	MB	Quebec	P.Q.	PQ
New Brunswick	N.B.	NB	Saskatchewan	Sask.	SK
Newfoundland	Nfld.	NF	Yukon Territory	Y.T.	YT
Northwest Territories	N.W.T.	NT			

In addressing mail to foreign countries, it is advisable to avoid using abbreviations, except the abbreviation U.S.S.R.

D. PLURALS OF ABBREVIATIONS

1. Plurals of abbreviations are usually formed by adding "s" to the singular form:

hr. hrs. Esq. Esqs. Dr. Drs.

2. If the abbreviation consists of *capital* letters, the plural is formed by adding "s" to the abbreviation:

R.N.s RNs C.P.A.s CPAs

3. For abbreviations consisting of *lower case* letters, add an apostrophe and "s":

c.o.d.'s cc's f.o.b.'s

4. Some single-letter abbreviations double the letter for the plural:

page = p. pages = pp.

5. Some abbreviations are the same for singular and plural forms:

ft. (foot, feet)   min. (minute, minutes)

E. POSSESSIVES OF ABBREVIATIONS

1. To form the possessive of an abbreviation in *singular* form, add an apostrophe and "s":

Frank Brown, Sr.'s office
The SEC's regulations

2. To form the possessive of a *plural* abbreviation ending in "s", add only the apostrophe:

Altman Bros.' sales
The CPAs' books and records

F. NUMBERS

1. Addresses

a. Numbers 1 through 10 are usually spelled out:

One Park Avenue
Two World Trade Center

Exceptions: R.R. 2
P.O. Box 9

b. Use figures for numbers over 10:

109 Los Angeles Drive
85 Fourth Avenue

c. The ordinal sign *st*, *d*, or *th* may be omitted so long as a word such as North, East, etc., separates the street number from the building:

475 East 18 Street

d. If no directional word intervenes, use the ordinal sign for clarity:

317-62 59th Avenue
2513 17th Avenue, N.W.

2. Time and Dates

a. Use figures with a.m. and p.m. The abbreviations a.m. and p.m. are usually *typed* in lower case, without spaces. In *printed* matter, they are typed in small capitals A.M., P.M. Do not use a.m. or p.m. with o'clock:

The ship will sail at 11:30 a.m.

The office closes at five o'clock
or 5 p.m. (*not* 5 p.m. o'clock)

The plane is due to arrive at 2 p.m.

In legal work the terminology is usually as follows:

The hearing will be held at ten o'clock in the forenoon of that day.

b. Time zones are abbreviated as follows:

Standard time	*DST Daylight saving time*	*or*
EST Eastern Standard Time	EDT Eastern Daylight Time	EDST
CST Central Standard Time	CDT Central Daylight Time	CDST
MST Mountain Standard Time	MDT Mountain Daylight Time	MDST
PST Pacific Standard Time	PDT Pacific Daylight Time	PDST

c. Days and months should not be abbreviated, except in statistical work when space is limited. In such cases the following abbreviations may be used:

Sun.	Jan.	Aug.
Mon.	Feb.	Sept. (Sep.)
Tues. or Tue.	Mar.	Oct.
Wed.	Apr.	Nov.
Thur. or Thu.	May	Dec.
Fri.	June (Jun.)	
Sat.	July (Jul.)	

In computer programming, "V" is sometimes substituted for "Th":

M T W V F

d. Well-known dates in history or graduation dates may appear in abbreviated form:

the 18th of April in '75   Class of '69

e. Decades may be expressed as follows:

The mid-1950s   1920s OR the twenties OR '20s

f. In a continuous sequence of numbers connected by a hyphen, the second figure may be abbreviated:

1975-78 OR 1975-8   pp. 261-4

If the first number ends in two zeros, the second figure is not abbreviated:

1800-1812   pp. 500-521

The second number cannot be abbreviated if it starts with different digits:

1880-1910   pp. 485-512

In numbers under 100, the second number is usually not abbreviated:

14-17 B.C.   pp. 75-77

3. Decimals and Fractions

Decimals

a. Decimals are always written in figures. A comma is used in the whole part of the number, but never in the decimal part. No space is left after the period:

4,768.275913

b. Spell out the word *cents* when the amount is less than **$1.** Spell out words denoting measures, capacities, financial quotations, etc., when they follow a number, unless the number is in statistical matter:

25 cents	9 miles
6 percent	93.5 average

c. A zero is usually placed before a decimal except when the decimal begins with a zero:

0.375 .0375

Fractions

d. Fractions standing alone are usually written out; fractions used as adjectives must be hyphenated:

She has a one-half interest in the estate.

One half of the class went to the museum.

e. Mixed numbers containing fractions should be typed with a space (not a hyphen) between the integer and the fraction:

45 7/8 *not* 45-7/8

f. If a fraction is the subject of a sentence, the verb agrees with the noun in the phrase:

Three fourths of the children's estates are taxable.

Three fourths of his estate is taxable.

g. The word *one* used with a fraction takes a singular verb:

One and two-thirds yards is the correct width.

4. Money

Following are some common abbreviations and symbols used to indicate money:

$	dollars	
¢	cents	
	pounds	
s.	shillings	5/ or 5s.
d.	pence	7 d.
%	percent	
fr	franc	
¥ or Y	yen	
2/10, n/30	2% ten days, net 30	
.50 or 50%		
$.75 or $0.75 or 75¢		

In legal documents, sums of money are expressed in words and repeated in numbers in parentheses:

Five Thousand ($5,000) Dollars.

The *plural* of numbers is formed by adding 's, except in stock market quotations or other instances, if preferred:

The order was for 100 IBM 5s at 493.
There are many 6's in stock.
Your address contains several 2s.

Large amounts of money may be expressed in numbers or words:

$5,000,000,000	5 billion dollars	*or*	$5 billion
$4,000,000	4 million dollars	*or*	$4 million

He owns $5,000,000's worth of property in the South.

When a whole dollar amount occurs in a sentence, it is not necessary to add a decimal point or ciphers.

Each heir will receive $25,000, approximately.

For uniformity in tabulation, two zeros are added to whole dollar amounts:

$46.57
50.00
1.83

5. Data Tables

Data means information (facts or figures) and is used in both a singular and a plural sense. When it refers to a *unit* comprising a number of facts, it is considered to be singular. The word *data* is a collective noun, the plural form of *datum* (Latin).

The data have been presented to the stockholders.

This data is not germane to the study.

Data is frequently presented in tabulated form. Careful planning is necessary because statistical material has to be arranged so that it is easy to read and appealing to the eye. It may be necessary to make a rough draft wherein the typist estimates margins, horizontal and vertical placement, and spacing between columns. A typist who finds it difficult to estimate can use either mathematical planning or the backspace method.

In tabulated reports the main heading is centered and usually typed in solid capital letters. Subheadings are typed with initial capitals for important words. Columnar headings are centered over the columns, with the first and important words capitalized. Headings may be underscored. Two particular points in tabulating are: (1) Clear all tab stops before setting stops for tabulation; (2) Tabulations should be typed line by line, not column by column.

In all tabulated material, *words* are aligned on the left; *numbers* are aligned on the right, with the exception of decimals:

Missouri	76	.33
Ohio	5,278	.0375
Alaska	430	.005

If the tabulation is extended, headings should be repeated on each page.

6. Roman Numerals

Roman numerals are frequently used to indicate volume, chapter, section headings and main headings. Most references to numbers require the use of Arabic symbols; some outlines combine the use of Arabic figures and Roman numerals.

I.
    A.
    B.
        1.
        2.
            a.
            b.
                (1)
                (2)
                    (a)
                    (b)
                        (i)
                        (ii)

Any intelligible system of outline notation is acceptable. Outside of technical narratives, legal pleadings, and thesis writings, there is little need for subordination beyond the second division of an outline.

Roman Numerals and Equivalent Arabic Symbols

I	1	XI	11	XXX	30	CCCC or CD,	400
II	2	XII	12	XL	40	D	500
III	3	XIII	13	L	50	DC	600
IV	4	XIV	14	LX	60	DCC	700
V	5	XV	15	LXX	70	DCCC	800
VI	6	XVI	16	LXXX	80	CM	900
VII	7	XVII	17	XC	90	M	1,000
VIII	8	XVIII	18	C	100	MM	2,000
IX	9	XIX	19	CC	200	MMM	3,000
X	10	XX	20	CCC	300	$\overline{V}$	5,000*
						$\overline{X}$	10,000*

*A dash above the numeral multiplies the value by 1,000:

$\overline{M}$ = 1,000,000; $\overline{V}$M = 6,000

1875 = DCCCLXXV
1978 = MCMLXXVIII
1994 = MCMXCIV
4000 = M$\overline{V}$

Combinations of Roman numerals are built by prefixing or annexing letters. The prefixing of a letter denotes subtraction and the annexing of a letter denotes addition:

44 = XLIV	L minus X and V minus I
69 = LXIX	L plus X and X minus I
76 = LXXVI	L plus XX and V plus I

Small Roman numerals are used in the preface of a book:

i	1	xi	11	xxi	21	liv	54
ii	2	xii	12	xxiv	24	lix	59
iii	3	xiii	13	xxix	29	lxi	61
iv	4	xiv	14	xxxiv	34	lxiv	64
v	5	xv	15	xxxix	39	lxix	69
vi	6	xvi	16	xli	41	lxx	70
vii	7	xvii	17	xliv	44	lxxx	80
viii	8	xviii	18	xlix	49	xc	90
ix	9	xix	19	l	50	xciv	94
x	10	xx	20	li	51	xcix	99

SUMMARY

Chapter 4 highlights some general rules for abbreviations and symbols. The keynote in the use of shortened forms is *consistency;* an abbreviation should not be used at one place in a particular document and spelled out in another. Included in this chapter are generally accepted abbreviations for titles, foreign expressions, companies, and geographic locations. Plurals and possessives of common abbreviations are also outlined. Reference is made to common usage of abbreviations and symbols in addresses, time and dates, decimals and fractions, and the indication of money. Also included are suggestions for using abbreviations in statistical data and for the utilization of Arabic symbols and Roman numerals.

Chapter 5

UNDERSTANDING FORMS AND USES OF CAPITALIZATION

The principles presented in this section should be of assistance in using capitalization correctly. While at times authorities differ on correct usage, it is helpful to become familiar with basic rules for capitalization. It is also advisable to consult up-to-date editions of good dictionaries; the GPO STYLE MANUAL, the United States Government Organization *Manual,* and other available style manuals.

Capitalization frequently poses problems in business because certain words may be capitalized in one situation and not in another; for example, words such as "common" and "preferred" stock, "court," order," "will," "codicil," "summons," "complaint," "affidavit," and so forth. When such words are used as titles or as names of legal papers or certificates, they are capitalized. In contextual material, capitalization is optional; the keynote is consistency.

Following are some basic rules for capitalization: Capitalize (1) certain specific words when used in direct reference to a proper noun; (2) the first word of a sentence; (3) proper nouns—names of persons, places, or things; (4) official and honorary titles; (5) words referring to the Deity; (6) each important word in a title (newspaper, magazine, book, etc.); (7) the beginning of each line of poetry; (8) the pronoun "I" and the exclamation"O"; (9) days of the week, months of the year, and the planets; and (10) the beginning of each quotation.

A. ERAS

Capitalize the names of historic eras and historical events:

Old World	Battle of Gettysburg
Middle Ages	Olympics
Renaissance	Fourth of July
Colonial Period	World War II

B. BUILDINGS

Names of buildings, hotels, and rooms begin with capital letters:

The Carlyle House
Hotel Ambassador
Windsor Suite

C. EDUCATION

1. Capitalize names of colleges, libraries, and educational agencies:

United States Office of Education
The College of New Rochelle
The Bayview Public Library
The Commission on Higher Education
The New York City Board of Education

but

a college education
a library book
an accrediting agency

2. Capitalize the abbreviations of academic degrees, but not the names of the degrees when combined with the word "degree":

B.A.	*but*	a liberal arts degree
M.S. in Mechanical Engineering		a master's degree in engineering
J.D.		a law degree
M.D., Ph.D., D.D.S.		a doctor's degree

3. A specific course of study is capitalized, but not the name of a field of study:

Trigonometry	a trigonometry test
Computer Applications	computer studies
Comparative Political Systems	course in politics

D. GOVERNMENT

Capitalize *Federal* and *State* when used with a definite name. Capitalize names of organizations and names of institutions on the national state and local level:

United States Congress	the House
Eightieth Congress	the Senate
United Nations	Supreme Court
Union of South Africa	
Federal Bureau of Investigation	

State Court of Appeals
Westchester County Court

Civil Court of the City of New York
Court of Claims

When the word "court" is used in a specific sense, it is capitalized; when used generally, it is lower case.

We refer to the mortgage now in foreclosure in the pending action in this Court.

He was held in contempt of court.

Capitalize routes, roads, and thoroughfares when they are part of a proper name:

Holland Tunnel	*but*	a tunnel
Staten Island Ferry	*but*	the ferry
Route 17 West	*but*	the western route
Interstate 280	*but*	an interstate highway

The name of a state is capitalized when part of a proper name, but not when it precedes the proper name:

Ohio State
state of Nebraska

Capitalization is optional when the name of the unit stands alone or is used as an adjective:

The respondent must produce all communications with officials of any municipal, state or federal government, or agencies or departments thereof, with respect to its work at the site.

but

The attorneys are working on the New York State Estate Tax return.

E. BUSINESS

1. Titles and Companies

Capitalize the words *board, bureau, department, division, service, office,* or *station* when referring to a particular section or when the name is given:

Board of Directors of the Crane Corporation
Bureau of the Budget of the City of New York
Sales Department
International Division
Foreign Service

Capitalize derivatives of proper nouns:

American	Italian
French	Roman

It is not necessary to capitalize proper nouns that have acquired common usage or independent meaning:

macadamized roads
diesel engine
dotted swiss
china (porcelain)

Capitalize a *title* preceding a name or when it is used with the corporation name:

President King will address the shareholders at the annual meeting.

The contract has been received from Mr. M. B. Lane, President of The Arax Corporation.

The communication from the President (or president) summarizes the situation.

Robert Smith, Esq. has been appointed a judge.

The names of companies are written according to the format of their incorporated title:

The First National Trust Company
B. Reinfeld & Company
Charles of the Ritz
Rhoda and Roger Creations
J. Marcel & Co., Inc.
Thompson Lane Hanrahan Caldwell & Landroth, P.C.

2. Business Reports

Capitalize words such as the following when they are used with figures or letters: *article, chapter, exhibit, model, number, policy, room, volume,* etc. The following divisions are not capitalized: *line, page, paragraph.*

> The State issued an approved order on contract as shown on Exhibit 65, Vol. VII, pp. 176-7.
>
> According to Article VI in Chapter 12, the item involved is Model 4-W, No. 8, located in Room 1006.
>
> Rebecca Jackson is the beneficiary of Policy No. 76524379.
>
> The testator disposed of his real and personal property in paragraph SECOND, lines 1 through 7, on pages 2 and 3 of his Will.

Capitalize the first word of an independent question or statement occurring within a sentence:

> She queried: Is that the reason?
>
> Brian said: "That's great."
>
> "That's true," she said; "You are correct."
>
> I am confronted with the question, Should I move with the Company to a new location?
>
> Should I move with the Company? is my question.
>
> *Note:* If a sentence contains a series of brief questions, which are not complete sentences, each question may begin with a lower-case letter:
>
> How was the weather on your vacation? the swimming? the sailing? the accommodations?
>
> If you decide to live in Europe, what will you do with your house? your automobile? your furniture?

Style books do not agree on the capitalization of hyphenated words. Two points should be kept in mind: (1) Capitalize any part that is a proper noun or adjective, and (2) use the selected style consistently:

The Corporation is moving its Sales Department to the North-East (or Northeast).

He is decidedly pro-American.

They will reside in the south-western section.

Political groups are capitalized, but not some of their derivatives:

a Republican
the Democratic Convention
the Labor Party
the Communist Society

but

a communistic form of government
a democratic approach

Capitalize the names of bills, laws, treaties, reports, etc., but do not capitalize common elements that stand alone in place of the name:

Trask Company Annual Report	*but*	an annual report
Panama Canal Act	*but*	an act
Bankruptcy Act	*but*	a bankrupt
Federal Rules of Civil Procedure	*but*	rules

3. Geographic Areas

Capitalize the words *earth*, *moon*, and *sun*, when they are associated with the names of other planets or stars. Capitalize the nine planets orbiting the sun:

Mercury, Venus, Earth, Mars, Jupiter, Saturn, Uranus, Neptune, and Pluto.

Astronomy classes include the study of Venus, Mars, and Earth.

After many days of rain, the sun was a welcome sight to the earth people.

Capitalize nicknames and imaginative names referring to persons, places, or things:

the Empire State	the Windy City
the First Lady	Iron Curtain countries

Do not capitalize words indicating general location within a state. Capitalize words that are actually part of the name:

western Montana	Southern Rhodesia
southern California	Northern Ireland

Capitalize such words as:

Northerner, Easterner, Westerner, Southerner.

Capitalize a word used to denote a definite region, locality, or geographical expression:

Orient, Far East, Near East, Middle West, the South, Middle Atlantic States, North Central States, the East, etc.

Capitalize words denoting geographic areas, but not these same words when they indicate direction:

He spends his winters in the South.

She is also going south this year.

The climate in southern France is balmy.

There is disturbance in South Africa.

They intend to drive north, east, south, and west on their tour of the United States.

4. Foreign names

Foreign parts of names are capitalized when not preceded by a given name or title:

the L'Amour family	Cardinal la Porte
the DeLeary business	Constance de Leary
Van Brederode	Jon van Brederode
the D'Amato home	Roberto d'Amato

Anglicized names are usually capitalized, except in a case of personal preference. There is no space between the particle and the remainder of the name:

O'Connor	McManus
MacDuff	FitzSimmons
VanDevere	VonCamp

Personal preference:

Nicholas duPont	Francis Dupont

5. Legal Documents

In legal documents such as agreements, motion papers and various pleadings, defined terms are written with initial capitals or in solid capitals depending upon the designation of terms. For example:

> This Agreement made the 28th day of July, 1980, between Margaret VanWurt (hereafter "SELLER") and JOHN and MARY CARTER (hereafter "PURCHASER") for the sale of property known and designated as 26 Albemarle Way (hereafter "PREMISES"). . . .

The words WHEREAS and RESOLVED are frequently included in legal papers.

WHEREAS, the parties have	RESOLVED, That the
WHEREAS a petition for	RESOLVED: That the

Note: The first word following WHEREAS is not capitalized; the first word following RESOLVED is capitalized.

F. RELIGIOUS DENOMINATIONS

Capitalize names of religions and their adherents, all names for the Bible, its parts and versions, other holy books, and words denoting the Deity.

Opinions differ with regard to capitalization of pronouns referring to the Deity. The consensus of writers is to capitalize *He* and *Him*, but not possessives, or to capitalize when necessary in order to avoid ambiguity:

God told Moses to lead *His* people.

Our Father (who) (which) art in Heaven, hallowed be thy name. . . .

Trust Him who rules all things.

Name of the Bible	*Names for the Diety*	
Old Testament	Father	Jehovah
New Testament	The Almighty	Saviour
Revised Standard Version	First Cause	Redeemer
English Revised Version	Divine Providence	Jesus Christ
Vulgate	Lord of Hosts	Holy Spirit
King James Version	King of the Jews	Son of Man
Douay Version	Holy Trinity	God

It is preferable not to abbreviate parts of the Bible when used in a sentence:

The story of Creation is found in Genesis, Chapter I.

Religious organizations and their adherents:

Christianity	Methodists	Pope
The Roman Catholic Church	Protestants	Holy Father
	Jews	Cardinal
Church of England	Catholics	Archibishop
High Church	Scriptures	Bishop
Episcopal Church	Gospels	Pontiff
Presbyterian Church	Jesuits	His Holiness
Church and State	Buddhists	Rabbi

Judaism	Moslems	St. Jude
Islam	Islamites	Virgin Mary

The "Benedictines never quit" is a slogan for an eminently successful school in the state of New Jersey which in the past has educated predominantly German Catholics, then Irish, Italian, and now black students.

Capitalize names of buildings, creeds, and professions of faith:

Cathedral of Cologne	Nicene Creed
Chartres Cathedral	Canon Law
Cathedral of St. John the Divine	Westminster Catechism
Westminster Cathedral	Lord's Supper

Capitalize: Devil, Evil One, Adversary, Father of Lies, Beelzebub

G. HOLIDAYS

Capitalize all names of *holy days* and *holidays*

Holy days	*Holidays*
Christmas	Labor Day
Easter	Fourth of July
Good Friday	Columbus Day
Yom Kippur	Memorial Day
Passover	New Year's Day
Ascension Thursday	Thanksgiving Day
Pentecost	Lincoln's Birthday
All Saints Day or Saints'	Washington's Birthday
Palm Sunday	Christmas
Ash Wednesday	
Chanukah or Hanukkah	

The months of the Jewish year are: (1) Tishri, (2) Heshvan (or Marcheshvan), (3) Kislev, (4) Tebet (or Tebeth), (5) Sebat (or Shebhat), (6) Adar (Adar Sheni added in leap years), (7) Nisan, (8) Iyar, (9) Sivan, (10) Tammuz, (11) Ab, and (12) Elul.

The period of fasting in the Christian Church known as Lent begins on Ash Wednesday, 40 days before Eastern Sunday (not counting Sundays). The last seven days of Lent constitute Holy Week, which begins with Palm Sunday. Passion Sunday opens Passion Week, which precedes Holy Week.

Holy Week culminates in Easter Sunday. In the second century A.D., Easter Day was the 14th of Nisan, the seventh month of the Jewish calendar. Christians in Europe observed the nearest Sunday. Easter varies between March 22 and April 25, and is the first Sunday following the Paschal full moon, which occurs upon or next after March 21st.

SUMMARY

Chapter 5 presents basic rules for capitalization, together with some illustrative examples. Included in the chapter are words relating to historic eras, modern buildings, the educational field, and government. Various areas of business activity are discussed, with particular emphasis on titles, corporate names, figures and letters used in business, capitalization of hyphenated words, the use of capitals in geographic areas, foreign names, proper names and derivatives in current usage, and common terminology used in legal documents. Reference is also made to religious denominations and holidays, and the use of capitalization in legal holidays.

Chapter 6

GUIDELINES FOR WORD DIVISION AND HYPHENATION

Business correspondence, memorandums, and data must be attractively arranged on the typewritten page. To this end, it is necessary to maintain approximately even margins in letters and statstical data; on legal-ruled paper, the material should be kept within the ruled lines. Excessive word division detracts from the appearance of the completed work, and an incorrectly divided word makes a letter unmailable. The secretary should be skilled in the correct division of words and she must use judgment as to when to divide and when not to divide words at the end of a typewritten line. In dividing words, the concept of readability must be kept in mind.

This chapter discusses some rules for word division and hyphenation. A knowledge and application of these rules should help the secretary develop a consciousness of when and how to divide words in order to save time and to assure the mailability of business material.

Guidelines for word division and illustrative examples are presented in the following pages.

A. WORD-DIVISION GUIDES

A fundamental rule in word division is not to leave more than seven spaces at the end of a line. This gives some leeway for word division; however, too many short lines should not occur together. Another basic rule is to type the first line of a letter or document to the end of the measured line and let that be a guide for the remainder of the page.

Following are some *specific guidelines:*

1. Divide words according to their pronounciation rather than their derivation:

knowl-edge	pro-duce	v.	pro-gress	v.
serv-ice	prod-uce	n.	prog-ress	n.
	prod-uct	n.		

2. Divide words only between syllables. Consequently, do not divide a one-syllable word:

length	thought	through	bridge
change	shipped	mailed	dates

3. Do not separate a syllable of one letter at the beginning or end of a word:

Type	along	amount	event	item	area
Not	a-long	a-mount	e-vent	i-tem	are-a

4. If possible, avoid dividing after a two-letter syllable at the beginning of a word:

Type	begin	design	enlist
Not	be-gin	de-sign	en-list

5. Do not divide words of four or five letters such as:

also	deny	data	very	enter
order	vital	oral	legal	copy

6. Do not carry over to the following line a syllable of one or two letters:

Type	fully	likely	ready	monthly	taken
Not	full-y	like-ly	read-y	month-ly	tak-en

Note: The hyphen would take the place of one letter, so it is useless to carry over any letter.

7. A one-letter syllable within a word should be retained with the preceding syllable and should not be carried over to the following line:

Type		*Not*
sepa- rate		sep- arate
regu- lation *or* regula- tion		reg- ulation *or* regul- ation
discontinu- ance *or* discon- tinuance		discontin- uance

8. Divide a hyphened compound only at the point of the hyphen:

Type	*Not*
self- confidence	self-confi- dence
re- cover (a chair)	re-cov- er
by-product *or* by- product	by-prod- uct
second- class	sec- ond-class

9. Divide a solid word only between two elements of a compound:

Type	Not
stock- holder	stockhol- der
semi- annual	semian- nual
inter- company	intercom- pany

10. Do not divide an abbreviation:

Litt. D.	Ph.D.	F.A.C.S.	U.S.S.R.
WABC	BPOE	NYSE	USA

11. When a final consonant is doubled before a suffix, divide between the doubled consonant, provided the last part of the word forms a separate syllable:

	Type	Not
running	run- ning	runn- ing
occurring	occur- ring	occurr- ing
putting	put- ting	putt- ing
setting	set- ting	sett- ing
recurring	recur- ring	recurr- ing
beginning	begin- ning	beginn- ing

12. When a suffix is added to a word that ends in a double letter, divide after the root of the word:

fill- ing	dress- ing	express- ing	sell- ing

13. The following word endings are not divisible:

-cal	-cial	-geous	-sial	-sion
-cle	-cian	-gious	-tial	-tion
-ple	-ceous	-gion	-tian	
-tle	-cious	-cion	-tious	

14. Do not divide a proper name:

Robert	William	Albert
Murray	Bertil	Evelyn
Alfreda	Nancy	Theresa

15. When two consonants come between vowels, divide the word between the consonants:

mes-sage	expres-sion
neces-sary	omis-sion
inter-roga-tories	cancel-la-tion

16. Avoid dividing numbers. If it is necessary to divide, divide at the comma and retain the comma. In a policy number, divide at the dash or diagonal, if any; if there is no break in the number, then carry the entire number over to the following line.

$4,475,582.55	$4,475, 582.55
Policy No. 6885823-75624	6885823- 75624
Policy No. 21385/764999A	21385/ 764999A

17. If it is necessary to divide a date, divide after the day and not after the month.

November 18, 1982	*Not*	November 18, 1982

18. Avoid separating the initials of a name and avoid separating initials, titles, or degrees from the name.

19. In printed material a dieresis is placed over a figure to indicate its pronunciation as a separate syllable from the preceding vowel, as in reënter. In typewriting, however, it is difficult to indicate the dieresis as this mark rarely, if ever, appears on a typewriter. Hence such words as reenter, cooperate, reelect, reenforce, etc., through common usage, are correctly written without the dieresis.

20. Whether or not a hyphen occurs after a prefix, it is preferable to divide the word only after the prefix:

anti-aircraft	antihistamine
anti-intellectual	semipublic
semi-invalid	semiweekly

The following simple rules should be kept in mind with regard to division of words at the end of a line:

a. Divide *only* when necessary.

b. Avoid dividing the last word in a paragraph.

c. Do not divide words at the end of more than two consecutive lines.

d. Never divide the last word on a page, except in legal documents when continuity may be necessary.

B. COMPOUNDS

A compound term is made up of two or more words joined together to convey a single idea. The term may be written together as one word, joined by a hyphen, or written separately but expressing a single idea; for example,

journeyman light-year vice president

Authorities and current usage do not agree on whether certain words should be written separately, with a hyphen, or joined together without the hyphen. Consistency is the keynote. What is done in one paragraph should be continued throughout a document.

It is recommended that up-to-date dictionaries be consulted with regard to current usage of compounds. Certain combinations of words take on a special meaning that the words separately do not have; through current usage such combinations have either become hyphenated or written as one word. One such example is: per cent. (Latin = per centum), per cent, and percent (current usage). Following are some suggestions in dealing with compounds:

1. Hyphenation

Compound adjectives are hyphenated because of the function they perform in a sentence:

This is an up-to-date typewriter.

Apparently the records are not up to date.

Secretaries have to update their address and telephone records of clients.

a. Hyphenate two or more words used as an adjective:

long-term loan	over-all coverage
above-captioned matter	tax-free bonds

b. When a noun is preceded by two adjectives, one of which is a comparative, superlative, or a color, the compound modifier is written without a hyphen:

a lighter work load	a light blue suit
the best known actor	dark red paint

c. When an adverb and an adjective precede a noun, no hyphen is used:

a likely enough excuse	a very beautiful child
a decidedly good course	a cleverly planned move

Note: Do not confuse "ly" *adjectives* with "ly" adverbs:

a friendly-seeming person
a costly-looking outfit
lightly-sounding footsteps

d. If a compound noun is preceded by an adjective that modifies only the first part of the compound, break up the compound:

taxpayer	income-tax payer
schoolboy	high-school boy
ballplayer	baseball player

e. Use a hyphen to unify a one-meaning adjective, whether the compound adjective comes before or after the noun:

An executive who is soft-spoken frequently gets his point across to his audience.

Many modern restaurants are remodeling with a decor that is old-fashioned.

It is advisable for some people to invest in bonds that are tax-exempt.

The effects of the news item are far-reaching.

f. Suspended hyphens are used in a series of compound adjectives having a common ending:

They are offering successive 5-, 8-, and 10-percent discounts.

The audience consisted of English-, French-, and German-speaking people.

g. Some commonplace adjectives are spelled as one word; other frequently used adjectives are used without a hyphen:

interstate moving	poverty stricken area
interoffice memo	consumer price index
semiannual report	horse and buggy days
subleased apartment	civil service examination
payroll office	real estate license
laborsaving device	public opinion poll

h. In a sentence which includes other modifiers in addition to a compound adjective, the independent modifier is not hyphenated:

The anniversary present was an expensive, last-minute gift.

We were accommodated in a reasonable, first-class hotel.

The treasurer delivered a detailed, cut-and-dried report.

i. When two nouns form into a single idea, the compound is usually not hyphenated, particularly if the first word is a monosyllable, or if the compound has only one primary accent:

airship	lawsuit
footnote	letterhead
passbook	leasehold
bathhouse	livestock
bookstore	postdate
goodwill	storeroom
shutdown	copyright

j. A noun formed by a short verb and an adverb is written without a hyphen, except when the solid form might lead to a miscomprehension:

		but
holdup	runoff	clean-cut
speechless	useful	run-on
gainful	otherwise	cut-in
livelong	crosswise	tie-line
wishful	districtwide	custom-made
hangover	businesslike	low-cost

k. Compounds beginning with the following monosyllables are usually written without a hyphen:

book	home	post	snow	tire
care	mind	school	speech	whole
eye	need	shop	sport	work

l. When nouns of one syllable are joined to the following word endings, the compound is not hyphenated:

straw*berry*	stead*fast*	house*keeping*
cherry*blossom*	corn*flower*	sun*light*
show*boat*	wheat*grower*	life*like*
text*book*	light*hearted*	sportsman*like*
air*borne*	share*holder*	end*long*
west*bound*	inn*keeper*	ship*yard*
hair*brush*	work*shop*	cock*tail*
business*man*	war*monger*	song*writer*
head*master*	home*ward*	over*time*
water*mill*	type*writing*	water*proof*
mouth*piece*		lock*smith*

Note: Many additional words fit into the above category.

m. Words beginning with *self* are usually hyphenated. Words that end with *self* are written as compounds without a hyphen:

self-made	oneself	ourselves
self-imposed	itself	yourselves
self-contained	herself	themselves
self-interest	myself	
self-insured	himself	
self-image	yourself	

n. Compass directions consisting of two words are written as one word; when three words are combined, use a hyphen after the first word:

southwest	south-southwest
northeast	north-northeast

In a proper name, the word is used as in the title: South-Western Can Company; North-eastern Service Corporation.

o. The words *any*, *every*, *no*, and *some* are written as solid words when combined with *body*, *thing*, and *where*. When *any* denotes a single person or thing, it is a separate word:

anything	everybody	nobody
anywhere	everywhere	nothing
nowhere	somewhere	somebody

Will *any* one of you volunteer to serve on the ad hoc committee?

Any thing you say will not be put on record.

p. Use a hyphen in writing out numbers from twenty-one to ninety-nine. Periods of time are generally expressed in words:

thirty-three-year old groom
twenty-four weeks
twenty hour flight
sixty-six trombones

q. Use a hyphen within a fraction, but omit it *between* a numerator or denominator:

twenty-five	twenty-five fortieths
thirty-one	thirty-one forty-fifths
fifty-five one-hundredths	three-fourths vote

r. A hyphen is used with figures expressing statistics or periods of time in technical measurements:

30-degree drop in temperature
50-50 chance
20-minute lecture
10-minute break
40-hour work week
25-year mortgage
4-day work week
15-day trial period (15 days' trial)
200-acre estate

s. Hyphenate coined phrases:

pay-as-you-go	drive-it-yourself	happy-go-lucky
better-off	up-to-par	run-of-the-mill
ready-to-wear	face-to-face	wall-to-wall
	red-penciled	

t. Hyphenate two or more words to indicate that a person or thing shares in more than one nationality:

French-Scotch-Irish	Italian-Greek
Anglo-Norman	Latin-American
Spanish-American	(*but* Latin America)

u. Use a hyphen after *ex*, *un*, and *all* in proper names:

ex-President Nixon
un-American
all-American basketball player

v. A hyphen is used in place of the word "to" to connect two figures that represent a sequence:

Articles I-IV
pages 19-25
week of July 17-23
during the years 1980-1985

Note: If the sequence is introduced by the words *from* or *between*, the hyphen is not used:
from 1975 to 1980
between 1912 and 1918

w. Use a hyphen when the words *elect* and *designate* follow a title:

President-elect   Ambassador-designate

x. A hyphen is used to join a single capital letter to a noun or participle:

T-square	X-ray	V-neck
H-bomb	X-raying	U-boat
		I-beam

y. In a compund modifier consisting of a foreign phrase, the hyphen is usually not used:

ex officio member	per diem employee
carte blance card	bona fide offer
a la carte menu	ad hoc ruling
prima facie case	guardian ad litem appointment

z. Do not hyphenate a title denoting a single office, but use a hyphen with a double title:

secretary general	secretary-treasurer
attorney general	president-manager
commander in chief	vice president-chairman
chief of police	
vice president	

2. Plurals of Compound Terms

Most compound nouns form the plural by pluralizing the principal part of the word:

	congressmen at large
vice presidents	governors general
trade unions	lieutenant governors
police captains	four-fifths
attorneys general	notaries public
by-laws or bylaws	court-martials

a. When the compound is made up of a *noun* and a preposition, a prepositional phrase, or an adverb, the noun is usually pluralized:

bills of lading	passers-by
works of art	runners-up
fillers in	brothers-in-law
lookers-on	listeners-in
	ambassadors-at-large

When a hyphenated compound does not contain a noun, pluralize the final element:

go-betweens	write-ups	shut-ins
hand-me-downs	tie-ins	
write-ins	run-ins	

c. When compounds are written as one word, the plural is formed according to the usual rules for nouns:

businessmen	cupfuls	handouts
leftovers	strongholds	letdowns
runarounds	holdups	bylaws
weekends	strikeovers	stockholders
stepchildren	hatboxes	bookshelves
courthouses	stepsisters	breakdowns

SUMMARY

Chapter VI discusses general guidelines for word division and hyphenation. Included in this chapter are 20 specific rules for division of words, prefixes, word endings, and numbers. Compound terms are discussed, with 26 guidelines presented for division of solid compounds and hyphenated compounds. Also included are rules for pluralization of compound words.

Chapter 7

SIMPLIFIED TECHNIQUES AND RULES FOR SPELLING

This chapter presents basic principles of spelling. Rules are suggested for spelling of words containing combinations of *i* and *e*, words ending in silent *e*, and in *ie*, and for doubling the consonant. Rules are also given for solving spelling difficulties with certain prefixes and word endings.

This chapter includes a list of 700 most frequently misspelled words. Selection of words is based on a study of test lists utilized by various business firms, by civil service, and by educational and research organizations in screening applicants for secretarial positions. Words included in this grouping are general in nature and do not represent any field of specialization. Division of the words herein was made with two ideas in mind: (1) how to divide a word at the end of a typewritten line; and (2) as an aid in the pronunciation of words.

Also included in this chapter is a list of words occasionally confused or misused. While the list is not entirely comprehensive, it does include words which may sound alike but are miles apart in meaning and which often pose a problem to secretaries. Reference to this section should alert the secretary to other words that are often confused or misused; for example, in a proper name such as San Diego or Santiago.

A. BASIC PRINCIPLES OF SPELLING

1. Using *e* and *i*

One of the most common difficulties in spelling is the combination of *e* and *i*. Even in typewriting, the transposition of these letters sometimes occurs since the *e* is struck with the second finger of the left hand, and the *i* is struck with the second finger of the right hand. The following rules should be helpful in the correct use of the vowel combinations *ei* and *ie*:

I before *e*
Except after *c*
Or when sounded like *a*
As in *neighbor* and *weigh*.

a. Use *e* before *i* after *c* (pronounced as *s*), when the sound is long *e*:

ceiling	deceit	receipt
conceit	deceive	receivable
conceive	perceive	receive
		receiver

Note: One exception is *financier*

b. Use *e* before *i* when *ei* is pronounced as long *e* (but not after *c*):

	plebeian	sheik
either	neither	seizure
leisure	seize	weird

c. Use *e* before *i* when the sound is short *i* (usually after *f* or *v*):

counterfeit	forfeit	surfeit
foreign	sovereign	

d. Use *e* before *i* when the pronunciation is long *i*:

Fahrenheit	seismograph
height	sleight

e. Use *e* before *i* when the pronunciation is long *a* (there are no exceptions to this rule):

		reign	their
deign	freight	rein	veil
eight	heir	skein	vein
feign	inveigle	sleigh	weigh
feint	neighbor	surveillance	weight

f. *ie*. Words that end with the sound *shent* or *shens* are spelled with *ie*:

conscience	patience	sufficient
efficient	quotient	transient

g. *ie*. When *i* and *e* are pronounced as two separate syllables, the pronunciation leads to correct spelling:

alien	recipient	experience
client	science	obedient
diet	scientific	
fortieth	furrier	*But*
hierarchy	seventieth	spontane*i*ty

2. Adding Word Endings

a. Words ending in silent *e* usually drop the *e* before a suffix beginning with a *vowel*:

accommodate	accommodating
advise	advisable

argue	arguing
bride	bridal
desire	desirous
exonerate	exonerating
guide	guidance
hope	hoping
ice	icing
judge	judging
owe	owing
sale	salable (or saleable)
use	usable
value	valuable
write	writing

b. Words ending in silent *e* sometimes retain the *e* before a suffix beginning with a consonant:

encourage	encouragement
false	falseness
hope	hopefully
issue	issueless
manage	management
nine	ninety
sincere	sincerely
whole	wholesome
wise	wisely

Exceptions:

abridge	abridgment
acknowledge	acknowledgment
argue	argument
awe	awful
due	duly
judge	judgment
nine	ninth
true	truly
whole	wholly
wise	wisdom

c. Final *e* is retained in words that could be mistaken for other words:

dye	dyeing
eye	eyeing
hoe	hoeing
shoe	shoeing
singe	singeing

d. Final *e* is usually retained before the suffix *age*:

acre	acreage
line	lineage
mile	mileage

Exceptions:

store	storage
use	usage

e. In words ending in *ie*, change *ie* to *y* when adding *ing*:

die	dying
hie	hying
lie	lying
tie	tying
vie	vying

f. Final *y*, preceded by a vowel, is generally retained before any suffix:

annoy	annoyed	employ	employs
attorney	attorneys	enjoy	enjoyment
betray	betrayal	essay	essays
boy	boys	money	moneys (or monies)
decay	decaying	obey	obeying
decoy	decoys	survey	surveyor

g. A word ending in *y*, preceded by a consonant, retains the *y* when *ing* is added:

reply	replying
spy	spying

But y changes to *i* when *ed* or *es* is added:

company	companies
lady	ladies
lonely	loneliness
reply	replied
spy	spied
theory	theories

3. Doubling Consonants

a. When adding a terminal beginning with a vowel, repeat the final consonant at the end of a single syllable if it is preceded by a single vowel:

abet	abetted
bag	baggage
club	clubbed
fat	fattest
fit	fitted
net	netting
plan	planned
wrap	wrapping

b. In adding endings, the final consonant is not doubled when it is preceded by two vowels:

proceed	proceeding
read	reader
scream	screamed
succeed	succeeded
sweet	sweetest

c. When a word ends in two or more consonants, the final consonant is not doubled to add an ending:

art	artful
fact	factor
mark	marking
tact	tactful
talk	talkative
yard	yardage

d. Words of two syllables, accented on the final syllable and preceded by a single vowel, usually double the consonant if the suffix starts with a vowel:

deter	deterrent
excel	excellent
forget	forgettable
infer	inferred
occur	occurrence
omit	omitted
prefer	preferred

e. At the end of a word, the final consonant is not repeated if the last syllable is unaccented:

catalog	cataloged
catalogue	catalogued
differ	difference

or if the accent shifts to the first syllable when the suffix is added:

defer	deference
prefer	preferable
refer	reference

f. Keep the double consonant at the end of a word when adding a terminal:

call	calling
forestall	forestalling
still	stillness

4. Word Beginnings

a. Word beginnings *ante-* and *anti-*:

These prefixes are sometimes confused because of meaning:

ante = before	*anti* = against
antecedent	anticlimax
antedate	anti-British
antenuptial agreement	anti-intellectual
anteroom	antithesis

b. Word beginnings *dis-* and *mis-*:

Confusion between dis- and mis- may be the result of a usage problem rather than a spelling problem:

dis = opposite or reverse	*mis* = badly or incorrectly
dis + like = dislike	mis + behave = misbehave
dis + please = displease	mis + fit = misfit
dis + satisfied = dissatisfied	mis + spell = misspell

Words formed by adding the prefix *dis-* and *mis-* are sometimes misspelled because of doubt about whether the combined form has one *s* or two. If the word to which the prefix is added begins with *s*, the combined form has two s's:

dis + seminate = disseminate	mis + spell = misspell
dis + service = disservice	mis + state = misstate
dis + similar = dissimilar	mis + step = misstep

5. Word Endings

a. Words ending in *c*: Add "k" to words ending in "c" when adding a terminal beginning with *e*, *i*, or *y*:

panic	panicky
picnic	picnickers
shellac	shellacking
traffic	trafficking

b. Words ending in *-sede, -ceed,* or *-cede*: Only one word in the English language ends in *-sede*: *supersede.* Three words end in *-ceed; exceed, proceed, succeed.* All other words end in *-cede:* (*Note: proceed* changes to *procedure*).

c. Adjectives of one syllable have two forms in the comparative and superlative:

cry	cryer	or	crier
dry	dryer	or	drier
	dryest	or	driest
spry	spryer	or	sprier
	spryest	or	spriest

Adjectives of one syllable usually retain the *y* before *ly* and *ness*:

dry	dryly	dryness
shy	shyly	shyness

The *y* is retained in compounds of -like and -ship and in derivatives of baby and lady.

ladylike	secretaryship
babyhood	ladyfinger

d. Words of a single syllable ending in *l* are usually spelled with double *ll*:

bill	fall	stall
call	hall	wall
cell	mall	well

Words of two syllables ending in *l* are usually spelled with a single *l*:

compel	normal	until
propel	rebel	willful *or* wilful

Some compounds of one-syllable words end in double *ll*:

carryall	install
enroll	overall
fulfill	uphill

e. Word endings *-able, -ible,* and *-uble*:

There are no definite rules stating when to use *-able* and when to use *-ible*. Words ending in *-able, -ible,* and *-uble* all mean *able to* or *suited to*. While *-able* is usually added to a complete word, and *-ible* and *-uble* are primarily added to root words, there are exceptions. The suffix *-able* is far more com mon than the suffix *-ible,* with about four-fifths of the words ending in *-able,* and one-fifth ending in *-ible*. Some basic principles are presented here, but it is recommended that a current dictionary be consulted when necessary.

-able added to complete word	*-ible added to root*
acceptable	eligible
agreeable	feasible
durable	flexible
imaginable	forcible
manageable	impossible
marketable	plausible
perishable	visible
	-uble added to root
	soluble

If a word has an *-ation* form, it frequently takes the suffix -able:

application	applicable
fashion	fashionable
presentation	presentable
quotation	quotable
reparation	reparable

If the base word ends in silent *e,* drop the *e* unless it is needed for pronunciation purposes. Note that *e* is needed to retain the sound before -able but not before -ible in the following words:

changeable	coercible
enforceable	convincible
foreseeable	defensible
noticeable	forcible

saleable *or* salable
serviceable
sizeable *or* sizable

plausible
responsible
reversible
sensible

Exceptions:

comparable
excusable
insurable
receivable
valuable

Words ending in *e* preceded by *c* or *g* do not drop the final *e* before the suffix *-able* or *-ous*, but do drop the final *e* before the suffix *-ible*:

manage	manageable	convince	convincible
service	serviceable	reduce	reducible
advantage	advantageous		
courage	courageous		

If the base word ends in *y*, change the *y* to *i* if it is preceded by a consonant, but retain the *y* if it is preceded by a vowel:

justify	justifiable	employ	employable
rely	reliable	pay	payable
try	triable		

If the base word ends in *ate*, the *ate* is dropped and replaced by *able*:

educate	educable
negotiate	negotiable
separate	separable
tolerate	tolerable

Some adjectives may be changed to adverbs by replacing the *le* ending with the adverbial ending *ly*:

credible	credibly
inevitable	inevitably
preferable	preferably
reasonable	reasonably
sensible	sensibly

f. Word endings *-ous, -us, -cial, -tial, -ance, -ence.*

(1) *-ous.* Many adjectives end with *-ous.* When adding *-ous* to a word ending with *y*, replace *y* with *e* or *i*, or drop it altogether:

beauty	beauteous
bounty	bounteous
miscellany	miscellaneous
envy	envious
industry	industrious
luxury	luxurious
melody	melodious
vary	various
infamy	infamous
monotony	monotonous

Silent *e* is usually dropped to add *-ous*, except when the *e* is needed for pronunciation:

continue	continuous	advantage	advantageous
fame	famous	courage	courageous
grieve	grievous	prestige	prestigious
nerve	nervous	outrage	outrageous

The ending *-ous* is added to a root word:

hazard	hazardous
humor	humorous
libel	libelous
vigor	vigorous

(2) Nouns usually end in *us*:

census	ignoramus
consensus	impetus
hippopotamus	

(3) Word endings *-cial* and *-tial:*

Nouns ending in *-ce* usually take *-cial* in forming the adjective; nouns ending in *-nce* take *-tial*:

artifice	artificial
face	facial
office	official
race	racial
circumstance	circumstantial
difference	differential
essence	essential
sequence	sequential

(4) Word endings *-ance* and *-ence*:

Nouns ending in *-ance* are usually formed from verbs ending in vowels:

ally	alliance
defy	defiance
endure	endurance
issue	issuance
persevere	perseverance

Exceptions:

maintain	maintenance
remit	remittance

Nouns ending in *-ence* are usually formed from verbs ending in consonants:

concur	concurrence
defer	deference
differ	difference
exist	existence

persist	persistence
prefer	preference
refer	reference

To form nouns from verbs ending in *-er*, drop the *-er* and add *-rance:*

encumber	encumbrance
enter	entrance
hinder	hindrance
remember	remembrance

g. Word endings *-cian*, *-cion*, *-sion*, and *-tion:*

(1) The endings *-cian* and *-cion* are usually added to words ending in *-c*:

magic	magician
music	musician
physic	physician
politics	politician
coerce	coercion

(2) Nouns derived from verbs ending in *-d*, *-de*, *-mit*, *-rt*, or *-ss* usually take the ending *-sion*; some words drop the *-d*, *-de*, *-s*, or *-t* before adding *-sion*:

admit	admission
collide	collision
commit	commission
convert	conversion
decide	decision
discuss	discussion
divert	diversion
extend	extension
recede	recession
transmit	transmission

(3) Nouns derived from verbs ending in *-ce*, *-m*, or *-te* usually take the ending *-tion:*

accommodate	accommodation
accumulate	accumulation
arbitrate	arbitration
compensate	compensation
depreciate	depreciation
discriminate	discrimination
exhilarate	exhilaration
fascinate	fascination
initiate	initiation
pronounce	pronunciation
redeem	redemption
renounce	renunciation
separate	separation

h. Word endings *-ise*, *-ize*, and *-yze* add the meaning "to do" or "to make" to the meaning of the base word.

(1) In general, *-ise* is added to a *root* word:

advertise	enterprise
advise	excise
apprise	exercise
arise	exorcise
chastise	franchise
circumcise	improvise
comprise	incise
compromise	merchandise
demise	premise
despise	reprise
devise	revise
disfranchise	supervise
disguise	surmise
	surprise

(2) The word ending *-ize* is usually added to a *complete* word; if the word ends in *-y*, drop the *-y* when adding *-ize*:

amort	amortize
apology	apologize

character	characterize
equal	equalize
item	itemize
jeopardy	jeopardize
memory	memorize
minimum	minimize
summary	summarize

(3) The ending *-yze* is added to few words:

analyze	electrolyze
catalyze	paralyze

B. 700 MOST FREQUENTLY MISSPELLED WORDS

ab′sence
absor′/bent
absorp′/tion
aca/dem′ic
accede′
accept′
accept′/ance
acces′/sible
acces′/sory
acci/den′/tally
accom′/mo/date
accom′/pany/ing
accord′/ance
accredit′ed
accrued′
ac′cu/racy
achieve′/ment
acknowl′/edg/ment
acquaint′/ance
acqui/esce′
accu′/mu/late
across′
adapt′
address′
ad′e/quate
adjust′/ment
ad′mi/ra/ble
advan/ta′/geous
adver/tise′/ment
adver/tis′/ing
advice′ (n.)
advis′/able
advise′ (v.)
advi′/sory
affect′
affi/da′/vit
ag′gra/vate
agree′/able
alleged′
all right
allot′
allot′/ment
allot′/ted
allow′/able
allow′/ance
al′most

alpha/bet′/ical
alread′y
alto/geth′er
alum′/nus
amend′/ment
among′
anal′/y/sis
an′a/lyze
announce′
announce′/ment
annoy′/ance
an′nual
ant/arc′/tic
antic′i/pate
apol′o/gize
appar′el
appar′/ent
appear′/ance
appli′/ance
ap′pli/ca/ble
ap′pli/cant
appoint′/ment
ap/prais′al
appre′/cia/ble
appro′/pri/ate
approx′i/mate
ar′chi/tect
ar′gu/ment
arrange′/ment
ar′ti/cle
ascer/tain′
as′i/nine
assess′/ment
assign′/ment
assis′/tance
assis′/tants
asso′/ci/ate
assured′
atten′/dance
atten′/dants
atten′/tion
attor′/neys
author′i/ties
autho/ri/za′/tion
au′tho/rize
aux/il′/iary
averse′

bac/ca/lau′/re/ate
banan′a
bank′/ruptcy
bar′/gain
ba′sis
begin′/ning
believe′
bene/fi′/cial
bene/fi′/ci/ary
ben′e/fited
bi′cy/cle
book′/keeper
breth′/ern
bril′/liant
bro/chure′
bud′/get
bul′/le/tin
buoy′/ancy
bu′reau
busi′/ness
busi′/ness/man
bus′y

cal′/en/dar
cam/paign′
can′/celed
can/cel/la′/tion

can′/not
cap′i/tal (chief; city)
cap′i/tol (building)
career′
cas′u/alty
cat′a/log
cat′e/gory
chauf/feur′
chim′/neys
choice
choose (to select)
chose (selected)
cir′/cum/stances
cli′/ent
cli/en/tele′
col/i/se′um
col/lat′/eral
col/le′/giate
colos′/sal
col′/umn
com′/ing
com/mence′/ment
com/mis′/sion
com/mit′/ment
com/mit′/tee
com/mu′/ni/cate
com′/pa/ra/ble
com/par′i/son
com/pel′
com/pelled′
com′/pe/tence
com′/pe/tent
com/pet′i/tor
com′/ple/ment
com′/pli/ment
com′/pro/mise
con/cede′
con/ceiv′/able
con/cern′
con/ces′/sion
con/cur′
con/curred′
con′/fer/ence
con′/fi/dent
con/fi/den′/tial
con/grat′u/late
con/nois/seur′
con′/science
con/sci/en′/tious
con′/scious
con/sen′/sus
con′/se/quence
con/sign′/ment
con/sis′/tent
con′/sul
con′/sul/ate
con/tin′u/ous
con/trol′
con/trol′/ler
con′/tro/versy
con/ven′/ience
con/ven′/ient
cor′/dially
cor/po/ra′/tion
cor/re/spon′/dence
cor/re/spond′/ents
cor′/ru/gated
coun′/cil
coun′/sel
coun′/selor
cour′/te/ous
cour′/tesy
cov′/er/age
cre/den′/tials

cred'i/tor
crit'i/cism
crit'i/cize
cul'/tural
cu'mu/la/tive
cur'/rent
cur/ric'u/lum
cus'/tomer
cyn'i/cal

debt'or
dece'/dent
deceive'
decide'
deci'/sion
deduct'/ible
defense'
defen'/dant
deferred'
defi'/ciency
def'i/cit
def'i/nite
def'i/nitely
del'e/gate
depen'/dent
depo'/nent
depo/si'/tion
depos'i/tors
describe'
descrip'/tion
desir'/able
dete'/rio/rate
deuce
devel'op
devel'/op/ment
device'
devise'

dif'/fer/ence
dig'/ni/tary
dilem'ma
direc'/tor
dis/ap/pear'
dis/ap/point'
disas'/trous
dis'/ci/pline
dis/crep'/ancy
dis/sat'/is/fied
dras'/ti/cally

ea'gerly
eco/nom'/ical
ec'stasy
edi'/tion
effect'
effi'/ciency
effi'/cient
elee/mos'y/nary
ele/men'/tary
el'i/gi/ble
elim'i/nate
embar'/rass
emer'/gency
em'pha/sis
em'pha/size
employee'
enclose'
endeav'or
endorse'/ment
en'ter/prise
enthu'/si/asm
envel'/op
en've/lope'
envi'/ron/ment
equip'

equip′/ment
equipped′
equiv′a/lent
espe′/cially
essen′/tial
et′i/quette
exag′/ger/ate
exceed′
excel′
ex′cel/lence
ex′cel/lent
except′
exces′/sive
ex′er/cise
exist′/ence
exor′/bi/tant
ex′pe/dite
expe/di′/tious
expen′/di/ture
expense′
expe′/ri/ence
expla/na′/tion
ex′tant
exten′/sion
extraor′/di/nary
extreme′ly

facil′i/ties
famil′/iar
famil′/iar/ize
fas′/ci/nate
fa′vor/able
fa′vor/ite
Feb′/ru/ary
Fili/pi′no
Fili/pi′/nos
fi′nally
finan′/cial
flam′/ma/ble
for′/ci/ble
fore/clo′/sure
for′/eign
fore′/word (preface)
for′/feit
for′/mally
for′/merly
forth′/right
for′ty
for′/ward (toward the front)
fourth
freight
friend
ful/fill′
ful/fill′/ment
fur′/ther/more

gauge
gen′u/ine
glos′/sary
gnaw′/ing
gov′/ern/ment
gov′/er/nor
gram′/mar
grate′/ful
grat′i/tude
griev′/ance
guar/an/tee′
guar′/anty

han′/dled
harass′
hard′/ware
haz′/ard/ous
height
hem′/or/rhage

hes'i/tant
hin'/drance
hono/rar'/ium
hon'/or/ary
hop'/ing
hy'giene

iden'/ti/cal
idi/osyn'/crasy
illeg'/ible
imme'/di/ately
imper'a/tive
impos'/si/ble
inad/ver'/tently
inas/much' as
in'cense (n.)
incense' (v.)
inci/den'/tally
incon/ven'/ience
incur'
incurred'
indebt'/ed/ness
inde/pen'/dent
in'di/gent
indis/pen'/sa/ble
indi/vid'/ual
induce'/ment
infal'/li/ble
influ/en'/tial
ini'/tial
in'quiry
in'quir/ies
insis'/tence
install'/ment
intel'/li/gence
inten'/tion
inter/cede'
inter/fere'

inter/rup'/ted
intrin'/sic
in'ven/tory
inves'/tor
irreg'u/lar
irrel'e/vant
i'tem/ized
itin'/er/ant
itin'/er/ary
it's (it is)
its (possessive)

jeop'/ar/dize
jour'/nal
judg'/ment
jus'/ti/fi/able

kimo'no
kimo'/nos
knowl'/edge
knowl'/edge/able

lab'o/ra/tory
led'/ger
leg'/ible
legit'i/mate
lei'/sure
length
let'/ter/head
li'ai/son
li'brary
li'cense
licen/see'
lien
lik'/able
lin'/eage
lin/guis'/tic
liq'/uefy
lit'/era/ture

live′/li/hood
loose (free from restraint)
lose (to be deprived of)

mag′a/zine
main′/te/nance
man′/age/ment
manu/fac′/turer
man′u/script
matric′/ulate
max′/i/mum
med′/ical
medio′/cre
memo/ran′da
memo/ran′/dum
memo/ran′/dums
men′us
mer′/chan/dise
mile′/age
min′/i/mum
mis/cel/la′/ne/ous
mis′/chie/vous
mod′/ern/ize
mort′/gage

nec′/es/sary
neg′/li/gi/ble
nego′/ti/ate
neigh′/bor/hood
nev/er/the/less′
nick′el (*or* nick′le)
nine′ty
ninth
no′tice/able
now′a/days
no′where (one word)

oblige′
obscene′
obses′/sion
obso/les′/cence
occa′/sion
occa′/sion/ally
oc′cu/pant
occur′
occurred′
occur′/rence
occur′/ring
offense′
of′fer
of′fered
of′fer/ing
offi′/cial
offi′/cially
omis′/sion
omit′
omit′/ted
or′di/nance (law)
or′di/nary
ord′/nance (munitions)
orga/ni/za′/tion
or′gan/ize
orig′i/nal
over/due′

paid
pam′/phlet
par/al/lel′
par′/tial
par/ti′/ci/pant
par/tic′u/larly
pa′tron/age
per cent (*or* per/cent′)
per′/ma/nent
per/mis′/si/ble
per/mit′/ted
per′/se/cute

per/se/ver'/ance
per'/sonal
per/son/nel'
per/suade'
per/sua'/sion
phase
phys'/ically
phy/si'/cian
pla'/gia/rism
plain'/tiff
plan
plan'/ning
play'/wright
pleas'/ant
plea'/sure
pos/ses'/sion
prac'/ti/cal
prac'/ti/cally
prac'/tice
pre/cede'
prec'i/pice
pre/ci'/sion
pre/fer'
pref'/er/able
pref'/er/ence
pre/ferred'
prej'u/dice
pre/lim'i/nary
pre'/mium
pre/req'/ui/site
pre/scribed'
pre/sump'/tu/ous
pre'/vi/ous
price list
prin'/ci/pal (chief; capital)
prin'/ci/ple (rule)
priv'i/lege

prob'a/bly
pro/ce'/dure
pro/ceed'
pro/ces'/sing
pro/fes'/sional
pro/fes'/sor
prom'i/nent
prom'/is/sory
pro/pel'/ler
pro/scribed'
psy/chol'/ogy
pub'/licly
pur'/chase
pur/su'/ant
pur/sue'
pur/su'er

quan'/dary
quan'/tity
ques/tion/naire'
qui'et
quin/tes'/sence
quite

real/ize'
re'ally
rea'/son/able
recede'
receipt'
receive'
re'cently
rec'/ipe
recip'i/ent
rec'/og/nized
rec'/om/mend
recur'
recur'/rence
refer'

ref′/er/ence
referred′
refer′/ring
regret′/ta/ble
reim/burse′
rel′e/vant
relin′/quish
reluc′/tance
remem′/ber
remem′/brance
remiss′
remit′
remit′/tance
renew′al
renown′
repel′
repe/ti′tion
rep/re/sen′/ta/tive
require′/ment
respect′/fully
respec′/tively
response′
respon/si/bil′i/ties
respon/si/bil′/ity
respon′/si/ble
res′/tau/rant
rhap′/sody
rhythm
ridic′u/lous

sac/ri/le′/gious
safe′ty
sal′/able
sal′/ary
satis/fac′/torily
sched′/ule
scis′/sors
secede′
sec′/re/tary
secu′/ri/ties
seized
sep′a/rate
serv′/ice/able
shep′/herd
ship′/ment
ship′/ping
siege
sig/nif′i/cance
sig/nif′i/cant
sig′/nify
sim′i/lar
simul/ta′/ne/ous
sin/cere′ly
sin/cer′ity
some′/one
some′/what
soph′o/more
sou′/ve/nir
spe′/cial/ize
spe′/cial/ties
spe′/cialty
sta/tion/ary (fixed)
sta′/tion/ery (paper)
stat/is/ti′/cian
sta/tis′/tics
stim′/u/lus
strict′ly
sub/mit′
sub/mit′/ted
sub/scrib′er
sub/stan′/tial
sub′/tle
suc/ceed′
suc/cess′/ful
suf/fi′/cient
su′ing

super/in/ten'/dent
super/sede'
su'per/visor
sup/ple/men'/tary
sur/prise'
sur/rep/ti'/tious
sur'/vey

tar'/iff
tem'/po/rary
ten'/ant
ten'et
their
there
thor'/ough
threw
through
through/out'
too
trag'e/dies
trag'/edy
tran'/script
trans'/fer
trans/fer'/able
trans/fer'/ence
trans/ferred'
trans/fer'/ring
trav'/eler
typ'/ing
ty'rant

ul'ti/mately
unan'i/mous
undoubt'/edly
unfor'/tun/ately
unnec'/es/sary
unpar'/al/leled

until'
ur'gency
ur'gent
us'able
u'sual
u'su/ally

vac'/uum
val'u/able
var'i/ous
veg'e/table
ve'hi/cle
ven'/dor
vicin'/ity
vis'i/ble
vol'/ume
vol'/un/tary
vol/un/teer'

ware'/house
weath'er
wel'/fare
whereas'
wheth'er
whole'/sale
wil'/ful *or* will'/ful
wil'/ful/ness *or* will'/ful/ness
with/hold'
worth'/while'
wrap
wrap'/ping
wrath
writ
writ'/ing

yacht
yield
yo'gurt

C. WORDS OCCASIONALLY CONFUSED OR MISUSED

(The definitions listed below are not all inclusive but are merely suggestions in order to clarify meaning. Consult a dictionary for comprehensive definitions.)

abjure	renounce solemnly; repudiate under oath
adjure	command; charge the jury
accede	agree
exceed	surpass
accent	stress
assent	agree
accept	receive
except	exclude
access	admittance
assess	levy
excess	surplus
act	a bill
action	legal proceeding
ad	advertisement
add	total
adapt	conform
adept	skillful
adopt	take
addition	increase
edition	publication
adverse	unfavorable
averse	reluctant; dislike
advice (n.)	counsel; information
advise (v.)	inform; notify; to counsel
affect (v.)	influence
effect (v.)	produce change
effect (n.)	result; outcome

agnostic	one who believes the existence of ultimate reality is unknown
atheist	one who denies the existence of God
aid	help
aide	assistant
aisle	passageway
isle	island
allowed	permitted
aloud	audibly; loudly
all ready	prepared
already	previously; by this time
all together	all in one place
altogether	completely; wholly
allude	refer to
elude	escape; evade
allusion	reference
illusion	false impression
altar	place for religious services
alter	change
alternative	choice in place of something else
choice	selected with care
always	constantly; all the time
all ways	in every way
amoral	being outside the sphere to which moral judgments apply
immoral	wicked
anecdote	story
antidote	remedy
angel	heavenly being
angle	figure formed by divergence of two straight lines
annexed	supplementary; added on

attached	connected; fastened; seized legally in order to force payment
anticipate	foresee
expect	assume; suppose; look forward to
any one	single
anyone	collectively
appellant	one who appeals
appellee	one against whom an appeal is taken
apperception	process of understanding something perceived in terms of previous existence
perception	awareness of environment through physical sensation
appraise	evaluate
apprise	inform
arbiter	a judge; one having power to decide
arbitrator	one chosen to settle differences between two parties in a controversy
arc	part of a circle
arch	curved part of a building
are	form of *be*
hour	time
our	pronoun
arraign	bring up on charges; accuse
arrange	organize; put in order
ascend	rise or go up
ascent	movement upward
assent (v.)	agree
assent (n.)	an agreement
assignee	person appointed to act for another; person to whom property is transferred
assigner *or* assignor	one who makes an assignment

assistance	help given
assistants	helpers
assume	pretend to have; take upon oneself
presume	expect with confidence; go beyond what is proper
atonement	making amends
attornment	tenant acting in capacity of landlord; or tenant getting new landlord although staying in same place
attendance	presence
attendants	escorts
atypical	irregular, not typical
typical	characteristic; belonging to a type
auger	wood-boring tool
augur	predict
aught	cipher; naught
ought	should
averse	unwilling; reluctant
avert	prevent; ward off
avocation	hobby; diversion
vocation	occupation; career
avoid	keep away from; shun
void	cancel; meaningless; empty space
avoidable	that which can be shunned
voidable	that which can be made to have no effect
bail	security
bale	bundle
balance	amount remaining; weighing device
remainder	that which is left over; balance
band	a group
banned	excluded; prohibited
bare	uncovered
bear	carry; animal

bases (plural)	foundations
basis (singular)	foundation
bazaar	market
bizarre	fantastic
because	for reason that
for	with purpose of; on behalf of
behind	in rear of
in back of	attached to rear of
berth	bed
birth	origin
beside	by the side of
besides	in addition to
between you and I	incorrect expression
between you and *me*	correct expression; object of preposition "between"
biannual	twice yearly
biennial	every two years
semiannual	twice a year
birth date	date when person was born
birthday	anniversary of birth
bloc	group of people
block	solid mass; piece of wood; platform
boar	male hog
bore	someone who tires you
boarder	one who pays for room and meals
border	a boundary
born	given birth (always in passive voice)
borne	carried (always in active voice)

bouillon	broth
bullion	gold or silver
brake	device; mechanism to stop vehicle
break	divide
breach	violation
breech	lower part
breadth (n.)	width
breath (n.)	respiration; air inhaled and exhaled
breathe (v.)	to take in air
bring	to carry to; to cause
take	to carry away from; to subtract
burned	past of *burn*
burnt	present participle of *burn*
buy	purchase
by	preposition
calendar	almanac; record of dates
calender	roller
colander	strainer
caliber	diameter; quality; measure of excellence
calibre	optional spelling of "caliber"
cannon	mounted gun
canon	law or rule
canyon	ravine
canvas	coarse cloth
canvass	solicit; search or examine
capital	chief; principal; city
capitol	building occupied by a legislature
carat	weight
caret	the symbol
carrot	vegetable

carton	box
cartoon	caricature
case	to inspect; lawsuit
cause	reason
casual	incidental
causal	arising; constituting a cause
casualty	accidental; not planned
causality	relationship of cause and effect
ceiling	top
sealing	closing
censer	vessel
censor (n.)	one who prohibits publication; critic
censor (v.)	to prohibit publication
censure (n.)	blame; disapproval
censure (v.)	to reprimand; disapprove of
cent	one penny
scent	odor
sent	past of *send*
choir	singers
quire	24 sheets
choose (v.)	to select (present tense)
chose (v.)	selected (past tense)
chosen (v.)	selected (past participle)
cite	quote; citation
sight	vision; view
site	location; place; foundation
situs	Latin—site
close	finish
clothes	garments
coarse	rough; unrefined
course	plan; school subject; way; path
collision	violent contact; accident; clash
collusion	secret agreement; fraud

colonel	officer
kernel	seed
comity	reciprocity; courtesy
committee	persons working together; group of people chosen
command	control
commend	praise
complement	complete; items which complete
compliment	praise; statement of praise
confidant (masc.)	friend
confidante (fem.)	friend
confidence	certainty
confident	hopeful
conscience (n.)	tells you right from wrong
conscious (adj.)	awake; alert
consistently	steadily; firmly
persistently	to go on resolutely in spite of difficulties
consul	foreign representative
council	assembly
counsel (n.)	advice given; lawyer
counsel (v.)	to give advice; to advise
contact	touch; association; connection
get in touch with	to get in communication with
continual	steadily recurring
continuous	unbroken; without interruption
contrast	to show differences when compared
compare	to examine for likenesses and differences; to represent as like something

core	center
corps	army; group of people
corporal (n.)	bodily; non-commissioned army officer
corporeal (adj.)	material; physical; bodily
correspondence	written communication
correspondent	one who writes
corespondent	one named jointly
cost	price; required expenditure
costs	damages of a legal action
costume	dress
custom	habit; taxes levied on imports
creak	noise
creek	stream of water
credible	believable
creditable	estimable; worthy of esteem
currant	fruit
current	up to date; flow of water; movement of electricity
cymbal	musical instrument
symbol	sign
decease	die
decedent	person who is dead
disease	illness
decent	upright
descend	move downward
descent	going down; ancestry
dissent (n.)	disagreement
dissent (v.)	to disagree
defendant	person required to answer in a legal action
dependent	relying upon; subject to another's jurisdiction

deference	respect
difference	variation
deferential	respectful
differential	varying
desert (n.)	geographical area; barren place
desert (v.)	abandon
dessert	food
device	invention; contrivance
devise (n.)	plan; disposing of real property by will
devise (v.)	to scheme; to prepare a method
devisable	part of an estate; can be passed on to heirs
divisible	capable of being divided
devisee	one who receives the bequest
devisor	one who gives property; who makes bequest
dice (n.)	used in gambling
die (n.)	tool used in shaping or stamping an object on material
die (v.)	cease to live
dies (n.)	plural of tool "die"
dies (v.)	third person singular of verb "die"
died (v.)	ceased to live
dye (n.)	material used for coloring
dyed (adj. or v.)	colored
dyes	colors
disburse	pay out; to allocate
disperse	scatter; break up
divers	sundry
diverse	unlike
do (v.)	to perform
due (adj.)	owing
dower	part of deceased husband's real estate which the law gives for life to his widow

dowry	wife's property; property that woman brings to her husband in marriage
drawee	person to whom promissory note or an order for payment is made out; one who receives payment
drawer	sliding container in furniture; person who makes a promissory note, or who draws an order for payment
dual	double; twofold
duel	combat; fight between two persons
dyeing	coloring
dying	expiring
egoism	doctrine holding self-interest to be the motive or valid end of action
egotism	excessive self-awareness; conceit
elicit	extract; call forth; extort
illicit	unlawful; not permitted
eligible	can be chosen
illegible	difficult to read; undecipherable
elude	evade; escape notice of
allude	to refer indirectly or by suggestion
elusive	baffling
illusive	deceptive
illusion	mistaken idea; fancy; misapprehension
emanate	arise; originate; come out from a source
happening	occurrence; take place by chance
emerge	rise out
immerse	to pluge into a liquid; to submerge; dip; to engross in thought
emigrant	person who leaves country to settle elsewhere
immigrant	person who comes into a foreign country and takes up permanent residence there

emigrate	leave country
immigrate	enter country
eminent	prominent; conspicuous; famous
imminent	threatening; ready to take place
envelop (v.)	to cover or enclose
envelope (n.)	enclosure used for mailing
ere	before
e'er	contraction for *ever*
err	mistake
eruption	outburst
irruption	sudden violent inroad or invasion; inburst
estop	prevent; prevent person from making denial or affirmation because it is contrary to previous affirmation or denial
estoppel	impedient raised by law
et al.	and others
et cetera	and so forth
extant (adj.)	still existing; existent
extent (n.)	range; degree of something
face	dignity; outward appearance; to confront blazenly
face up to	incorrect expression
facility	aptitude; ease in performance; something built to serve a purpose
faculty	power; ability to act or do; members of a profession
faint	collapse
feint	pretend
fair	pleasing
fare	fee
farther	distance; more completely
further	advance; in addition; reference to time

faze	to disturb; daunt
phase	aspect
feat	act of skill
feet	plural of *foot*
fictional	invented by the imagination
fictitious	imaginary; legendary
finally	lastly
finely	excellently
fiscal	financial
physical	material
forceful	violent; strength of high degree
forcible	showing energy; obtained by force
formally (adj.)	ceremoniously
formerly (adv.)	hitherto; earlier time
forth	onward; forward
fourth	after third
foul	unfair
fowl	bird
freeze	congeal; harden into ice
frieze	ornamental border extending around a room or a building
gamble	speculate
gambol	play
gap	opening
gape	stare
gilt	like gold
guilt	wickedness
gist	pith; main point of a matter
jest	joke

grate	frame
great	large
grill	broil
grille	metal fence
guarantee	pledge; undertake an obligation
guaranty	contract; security; undertaking to answer for another's failure to pay a debt
guessed	conjectured; surmised
guest	visitor
handsome	beautiful
hansom	carriage
heal	cure
heel	part of foot
hear	listen
here	this place
hearsay	rumor
heresy	opposing opinion
hew	cut
hue	color
higher	above
hire	employ
hoard	amass
horde	tribe
hole	opening
whole	entire
holy	sacred
wholly	entirely
human	pertaining to people
humane	pertaining to compassion or kindness
ignorant	lacking knowledge; unaware
illiterate	unable to read or write

implicit	understood
explicit	clearly expressed
imply	suggest; hint at; express indirectly
infer	surmise; guess; derive as a conclusion from facts or premises
inapt	not suitable
inept	foolish; absurd
incidence	range of occurrence
incidents	events
incite	arouse
insight	understanding
indict	accuse
indite	compose; to put in writing
ingenious	clever
ingenuous	frank; open; artless
in re	regarding the matter; in reference to
in rem	in the action [against the thing and not the person]
instance	occasion
instants	moments
interpellate	question formally
interpolate	interject a remark; insert into a text or conversation
interstate	between or among states
intrastate	within one state
irregardless	no such word
irrespective	without regard to
its	possessive pronoun; belonging to it
it's	it is
judicial	ordered or enforced by a court; relating to administration of justice

judicious	wise; discreet; characterized by sound judgment
jura	justice; entire body of law (jus, singular; jura; plural)
jurat	clause at bottom of affidavit stating when, where, and before whom the affidavit was signed
knew	past of *know*
new	recent
know	perceive directly; recognize
no	negative; not so
later	after a specified time
latter	the last one mentioned
lead	metal (pron. *led*); to conduct (pron. *leed*)
led	guided (past of *lead*)
lean	think; rely on; incline
lien	legal claim upon property for the satisfaction of a debt or duty
leased	rented under contract
least	smallest
lessen	diminish
lesson	instruction
lesser	inferior
lessor	landlord
liable	accountable; responsible
libel	printed statement which is untrue or which injures a person's good name
lightening	relieving of a load; to enlighten
lighting	illuminating; igniting
lightning	discharge of light caused by passing of electricity from one cloud to another or from a cloud to the earth

load	quantity; burden
lode	mineral deposit
loan	something lent or borrowed
lone	one
loath	unwilling; reluctant
loathe	detest; hate
local	sectional; relating to one place
locale	locality
loose (adj.)	not tight
lose (v.)	to misplace; to be defeated
magnate	person of rank
magnet	lodestone; power to attract
malfeasance	performance by a public official of an act that is contrary to law
misfeasance	the wrongful performance of a normally lawful act
nonfeasance	omission of some act which ought to have been performed
manner	mode
manor	mansion
mandatary	person or nation holding a mandate; bailee to whom goods are delivered
mandatory	compulsory; authoritatively ordered
marital	pertaining to marriage
martial	military; warlike
marshal	officer
material	goods; any constitutent element of a thing
materiel	equipment; aggregate of "things" used in any business (distinguished from "personnel")
may	permission; possibility; opportunity
can	have ability; know-how; means to

maybe	perhaps
may be	possibly may occur
mean	average; to signify; to intend
mien	manner
medal	reward
meddle	interfere
metal	ore; crushed stone
mettle	courage; spirit
miner	worker in a mine
minor	under age
monetary	financial
monitory	warning
moneys *or* monies	pecuniary sums; funds; cash
moral	ethical; concerned with right conduct
morale	spirit; mental or moral condition
morning	early day
mourning	grief
motif	theme; main feature of work of art; music, literature, etc.
motive	reason; idea; need
notorious	widely but unfavorably known
famous	celebrated; renowned
ordinance	decree; especially a local law
ordnance	cannon; artillery
over	finished; above in place or position
more than	in excess of; above in degree, quantity
overdo	overwork
overdue	delayed beyond the proper time for payment
pain	hurt; suffering; sorrow
pane	sheet of glass in door or window

pair (n.)	two of a kind
pare (v.)	to peel
pear (n.)	fruit
partition	division; separation; division of property among joint owners
petition	formal request; to request or solicit
party	one of the litigants in a legal proceeding; person or group that participates in some action
person	the actual self or individual personality of a human being
passed	past tense and past participle of *pass*
past	gone by; earlier time
patience	calm endurance
patients	people under medical care
payee	one in whose favor a check, note, etc. is drawn
payor	one who makes payment
peace	calm; not war
piece	part of
pedal	lever worked by feet
peddle	offer for sale from place to place
persecuted	ill-treated; pesistently harassed; punished for adherence to principles
prosecuted	sued; followed up and completed
personal	private; pertaining to oneself
personnel	staff; employees of an organization
perspective	mental aspect; true relationship of objects or events to one another
prospective	expected; hoped for
plain	unadorned; simple; easily understood
plane	level; flat
plaintiff	accuser
plaintive	mournful

practicable	feasible; capable of being done with available means
practical	useful; matter-of-fact
precede	go before; preface
proceed	go ahead; to continue any action or process
precedence	priority in rank importance; time; diplomatic protocol
precedent	standard; legal decision serving as an authoritative rule in future similar cases
president	head
prescribe	to lay down rules; to direct; to render invalid by prescription
proscribe	to denounce; prohibit; to banish or exile
presence	attendance; immediate vicinity; personal appearance or bearing
presents	gifts; the present writings used in a deed, a lease, etc., to denote the document itself
principal (n.)	head of a school; money owned; capital; a person who authorizes another, as an agent, to represent him; chief actor in a play
principal (adj.)	chief; most important
principle (n.)	a rule or doctrine; theory
profit	gain
prophet	foreseer
prophecy	prediction
prophesy	to foretell
propose	suggest
purpose	intention
queue	braid of hair; file or line of people waiting their turn

cue	a hint; long rod, tipped with leather, used to strike the ball in billiards
quiet (adj.)	not noisy
quite (adv.)	almost completely
raise	lift
rear	hindmost portion; take care of and support up to maturity
rays	beams
raze	destroy
rise	to become prominent; to become animated; to get up from a lying or sitting position
rap	knock
wrap	enclose
reality	truth
realty	real estate
recurring	appearing again; repeatedly
frequent	happening at short intervals; habitual
refute	to prove to be false or erroneous
deny	to state that something is not true
reign	rule
rein	halter
reiterate	to say again
repeat	to reproduce sounds; utterances, etc.
residence	home
residents	persons
return	due date; return date of an order or summons
writ	a writing; a formal document under seal, issued in the name of a court, expressing an order or command
right	correct
rite	ceremony
wright	worker

write	express visually
role	a part
roll	a list
roomer	a lodger
rumor	hearsay
root	part of a plant
route	a course or path
seize	grasp
siege	battle
sense	meaning; ability to think well
since	before this time; because
serial	sequential
cereal	food
session	conference
cession	yielding
shear	to cut
sheer	thin
sight	vision; view
site	position, place
situate	position of property; in a particular site
situated	placed in a particular position or condition
sleight	artful
slight	trivial
stationary	stable; in a fixed position
stationery	paper
statue	image
statute	law
status quo	existing state or condition
in statu quo	keep things as they are
stile	barrier
style	fashion

straight	unbroken
strait	narrow pass
suit	legal proceeding; clothing
suite	matched group
sweet	having a taste of sugar
superintendence	management
superintendents	supervisors
tail	appendage; rear end of animal
tale	story
tare (n.)	weight; allowance
tear (v.)	to rip
than	used to compare things; in comparison
then	at that time; indicating time
their	belonging to them
there	in that place
they're	they are (contraction)
therefor	for it; in exchange for that or this
therefore	consequently; thus; for that reason
therein	in that matter, circumstance; etc.
thereof	from or out of that origin or cause
thereon	thereupon; immediately after that
threw	past tense of throw
through	between the parts of; by means of
tier	row or layer
tear	drop of fluid
to (prep.)	indicating direction
too (adv.)	excessively; also
two (n.)	number; 1 + 1
topography	geographical
typography	from type

tortious	wrongful; pertaining to a civil wrong
tortuous	evasive; devious; roundabout; morally crooked
track	footprint
tract	treatise
trail	a rough path
trial	experimental action; examination before a court
transferee	a person to whom a transfer is made, as of property
transferor	a person who makes a transfer, as of property
vendee	the person to whom a thing is sold
vendor	a person or agency that sells
vice (n.)	immorality
vise (n.)	devise for holding
vise (v.)	to hold or squeeze
waist	bodice
waste	refuse
waive	set aside
wave	signal
ware	goods
wear	clothe
where	whither
weather	state of the atmosphere
whether	expressing alternatives
which	what one "which of these do you want?" "You may choose which you like."
that	used to indicate one of two or more persons or things already mentioned: "That is her father."

Note: "which" is used to introduce nonrestrictive relative clauses: "The boat, which has a diesel engine, has been sold."

"that" is used to introduce restrictive relative clauses:
"The boat that has a diesel engine has been sold."

who's	who is (contraction)
whose	belonging to whom; possessive of *who*
you're	you are (contraction)
your	belonging to you; possessive of *you*

SUMMARY

Chapter 7 discusses techniques and rules for spelling. Basic principles are suggested for solving spelling difficulties with various combinations, and for the use of certain prefixes and suffixes. Included in the chapter is a list of 700 most frequently misspelled words. Also included is a list of words occasionally confused or misused.

Chapter 8

A PRACTICAL GUIDE TO EFFECTIVE BUSINESS LETTERS

A letter sent by a business firm is a graphic representative of that firm. Most companies purchase high-quality bond paper and have the company name, logo, and names of executives attractively placed on the paper—usually engraved. The secretary must be able to produce an attractive, well-balanced letter, free from any noticeable corrections. The correcting device on modern typewriters is of great assistance in typing an attractive letter, but the effect of balance requires judgment on the part of the typist.

While shortcuts in correspondence are gradually being introduced, particularly with the advent of the AMS Simplified Style, most businesses continue to use the standard letter styles employing the following components: heading, date, inside address, salutation, body, complimentary close, signature, identifying initials, enclosure notation, and, when pertinent, the attention and reference or subject lines. In legal correspondence, the reference matter is practically always included.

This chapter deals with various styles of business letters and memorandums, punctuation, salutation, complimentary closings, and signature lines.

A. THE BUSINESS LETTER

Most business letters are typed on standard paper (8½″ × 11″) of good bond quality, usually containing a watermark and an engraved letterhead. Personal and professional letters are often typed on what is commonly known as "Monarch" size paper (7¼″ × 10½″). Placement of letters is based largely upon their length, also taking into consideration variation in letterheads, content, structure, and style. Each letter must be treated as an individual problem, and letter placement should become an intuitive process.

The date is typed about three lines below the letterhead. Spacing between the date and inside address depends upon the length of the letter: Leave space of 4 lines after the date for a long letter, 6 lines for a medium letter, and 8 lines for a short letter. When an attention line or a subject matter reference is included, allowance should be made for such items. Handbooks in many offices stipulate that 1½″ margins should be maintained on the left and right side, and also on the bottom of the paper. Whether the typewriter has elite or pica type, the 1½″ *white* margin is a good guide for proper placement. For a very short letter, of course, the bottom margin would be greater. The 1½″ margin rule is a helpful guide not only in achieving balanced letters, but also in achieving balanced reports and memorandums. When typing a letter on the Monarch size stationery, the *white* margin can be reduced to 1¼″ or 1″, depending upon the length of the letter.

B. PARTS OF THE BUSINESS LETTER

Business letters are ordinarily typed on letterhead stationery that contains the name and address of the firm and frequently the names of the chief executives or partners.

In typing personal letters on plain paper, the return address may either be centered about one-inch from the top of the paper, or by starting the return address at the center of the paper about 1½ or 2 inches from the top of the paper:

522 Douglass Parkway
Westfield, New Jersey 07090

or

522 Douglass Parkway
Westfield, New Jersey 07090

1. Date Line

The month is always written in full; the day is written in figures followed by a comma and the year; for example, December 8, 1982. Never use the style 12/8/82 since this could be misinterpreted by foreign correspondents as the 12th day of August, 1982.

The endings *th, nd, st,* and *d* are sometimes used after numbers when the number is not followed by the *year,* or in legal documents when the day precedes the month. For example:

> We sent you a notice on May 15th and again on June 15th, but we have had no response from you to date.
>
> Sworn to before me this 22nd day of July, 1980

2. Notations

Mailing notations, personal and confidential notations, and other notations are usually typed about two lines below the date of the letter, at the left margin:

SPECIAL DELIVERY

CERTIFIED MAIL
RETURN RECEIPT REQUESTED

REGISTERED MAIL

PERSONAL AND CONFIDENTIAL

3. Inside Address

The inside address begins at least 3 lines after the notation, if any, or 4-5 lines or more after the date, depending on the length of the letter. An inside address is usually single spaced, whether the letter is single or double spaced.

a. Names and Titles

It is the consensus of some businessmen that two titles should not be typed on the same line, reasoning that the company title belongs with the company name:

Mr. Frank Larkin
President, Mullen Corporation

not

Mr. Frank Larkin, President
Mullen Corporation

When the name of the corporation is lengthy, such an arrangement would not be appropriate. In such case, the title is typed on a separate line:

Mr. Roy Baldwin
President
Acme Construction Corporation

or (for balance)

Mr. Roy Baldwin, President
Acme Construction Corporation

and

Mr. Alexander Whitehall
Vice President and
General Counsel
Acme Construction Corporation

In the following instances, the title *Mr.*, *Mrs.*, *Ms.*, or *Miss* is not used:

Christine Giblin, M.D.
Robert Fitzsimmons, Ph.D.
James Carroll, Esq.
Evelyn Delaney, D.D.S.

The concept of balance and the exercise of good judgment are requisite for the correct placement of an inside address. It is of the utmost importance to pay strict attention to detail in the typing of personal names and company names, which should be spelled out or abbreviated exactly as shown on the stationery of the respective company. At times it is necessary to make a telephone call in order to ascertain the correct spelling of a name.

b. Street Address

Room numbers and names of buildings are sometimes included in the address. The name of the building should be typed on one line, and the address on the other. For example:

Suite 222, Parker Building
40152 Madison Avenue
Tulsa, Oklahoma 74107

Street addresses in Washington, D.C., Atlanta, Georgia, Seattle, Washington, and other cities have direction abbreviations after the street names, which must be placed on the same line as the address:

2460 Massachusetts Avenue, N.W.
1788 16th Avenue, S.E.

c. Cities and States

Never use an abbreviation for a city, such as Chic. for Chicago, or N. Y. for the city of New York. The following abbreviations are acceptable: St. Louis, Mt. Vernon, Ft. Benning, Pt. Pleasant, and so forth. It is always preferable to spell out such words as: Fort Monmouth, Treasure Island, Point Lookout, and similar names.

The name of the state may be abbreviated or spelled out according to the writer's preference. The two-letter state abbreviations formulated by the United States Post Office are recommended for speed and efficiency, but when used these two letters must be followed by the zip code identification. In a foreign address, the name of the country should be typed in solid capitals: JAPAN, FRANCE, U.S.S.R., KENYA, etc.

4. Attention Line

The attention line is written between the inside address and the salutation. In present practice it is usually written as follows: Attention: Mr. George Busch. Either the salutation "Gentlemen" or "Dear Sirs" is correct because the letter is directed to the firm but to the special attention of a certain person. Frequently, however, the dictator says: "Dear Mr.—." The secretary should type the form that is dictated.

5. Salutation

The following are the most common forms for business letters: (Use either open punctuation or place a colon after the salutation.)

Dear Sirs
Gentlemen
Dear Mr. Jones:
Dear Mrs. Jones:
Dear Ms. Jones:
Dear Miss Jones:
Ladies: (if it is known that the organization consists of women only)

Businessmen often use first names when dictating letters, particularly if they have been dealing with the person over a period of time.

If the individual name of a person is not known, the letter may be addressed to the position that person holds:

Secretary Seaview Corporation (address)	President The Wilson Men's Club (address)
Dear Sir or Madam:	Dear Sir: *or* Dear Sir

In addressing partners in a firm, the usual form is:

Black and Brown, Esqs. 46 Pyne Street New York, N. Y. 10028 Attention: Mr. William Black	William Black, Esq. Messrs. Black and Brown 46 Pyne Street New York, N. Y. 10028
Gentlemen: *or* Dear Sirs: *or* Dear Mr. Black	Dear Mr. Black: *or* Dear Sir:

In a letter containing *mixed* punctuation, a colon follows the salutation; in a letter containing *open* punctuation, no mark follows the salutation.

In a *personal* letter, a comma always follows the salutation:

Dear Alice, Dear Kenneth,

6. Subject Line

The subject or reference matter may be centered above or below the salutation, but preferably as close as possible to the body of the letter. The subject matter is quite frequently introduced with *Re:*, *Subject:* or without an introductory word. Reference material may consist of one, two, three or more lines.

In legal correspondence, the reference line is practically a *must*. Insurance, banking, or tax letters usually carry a reference to a policy number, account number, or case number.

7. Body of the Letter

The body of the letter may be written either in block form or indented form. Short letters sometimes consist of one paragraph. Medium and long letters have a beginning, a middle, and an ending. Most writers give particular consideration to the opening and closing paragraphs. The middle paragraphs should be sequential in structure so that the flow of thought may be comprehended. The middle paragraphs in a letter are often quite numerous. In composing business letters, the elements of clarity, conciseness, correctness, and courtesy are goals which business writers try to keep in mind.

8. Complimentary Close

The complimentary closing is typed two lines below the last line of the letter. In a block-form letter it is typed at the left margin; in a modified block-form letter, the closing begins at the right of the vertical center. The selection of the complimentary close depends upon the tone of the letter and relates to the salutation.

If "Gentlemen" or "Dear Sir" is used, the closing is usually:

Very truly yours *or* Yours very truly

When "Dear Mr. —", "Dear Philip", "Dear Ms. —", etc., are used, the closing may be:

Sincerely, Sincerely yours, Cordially, Cordially yours, etc.

Note: Only the *first* word of the complimentary closing is capitalized.

Writers frequently use a participial phrase in the form of a greeting before a complimentary closing. For example: "Looking forward to seeing you in Chicago"; "Trusting your family is well"; "Thanking you for your courtesy"; etc. Such statements could be changed to complete sentences, but they should be typed as dictated unless there is an understanding that the secretary may change the sentence structure.

9. Signature Line

The most common form of signature in business letters today is to write the title of the person four/five lines after the complimentary close; if the person's name is typed, then the title is typed on the line following the name. When writing opinion letters, attorneys usually have the firm name typed first, followed by the name of the person who actually wrote the letter. Frequently the name of a corporation is also written in the signature section. If the name of the writer appears in the heading section of the letter, some writers prefer that no name or title appear in the signature section.

When the company name is used in the closing lines, it should be typed two spaces below the complimentary close, followed by the name of the dictator and/or his official position four spaces below the company name:

Very truly yours, ANTRIM CORPORATION B. Martin Black President	*or*	Yours very truly ANTRIM CORPORATION By: ____________________ Bert Brant, Sales Manager

Very truly yours, James R. Townsend	Yours very truly Vice President and General Counsel

At least one given name should be typed out in full. It is considered poor form to use *one initial* only in an address or a signature line, although two initials are acceptable.

Signatures for women vary according to status and preference. When only a handwritten signature is used, the title should be enclosed in parentheses; when the name is typed beneath the signature, the title need not be enclosed in parentheses:

Sincerely yours,

(Miss) Constance Sherman

Sincerely yours

Constance Sherman

Miss Constance Sherman

The manner in which a married woman signs her name is determined by whether the purpose is social or business. For example: Mary Cox becomes Mrs. James Martin (through marriage).

Socially, she could sign:

Mary Cox Martin (her actual name)

(Mrs. James Martin) (her title)

On checks, she would sign:

Mary Martin;

Mary C. Martin; or

Mary Cox Martin

Legally, she would be designated as "Mary Cox Martin" a/k/a (also known as) Mrs. James Martin; or if she prefers not to retain her maiden name, then she is "Mary Martin a/k/a Mrs. James Martin."

A widow should sign her name exactly as she did before the death of her husband:

Mary Martin (her name)
Mrs. James Martin (her title)

It is proper for a widow to retain her husband's title.

Some professional women prefer to keep their maiden name:

Grace Hanson, M.D.
(Mrs. Stephen Moore)

A woman who is divorced has the choice of assuming her maiden name, with or without the title "Mrs." *or* she may retain her husband's surname with "Miss" or "Mrs." Socially she would be known as "Mrs. Grace Moore"; but, if divorced, she may not use her former title as "Mrs. Stephen Moore."

A private secretary may add her own initials when she signs her employer's name, or she may sign her own name adding the word "for" with the employer's name:

Anthony Pratt
H. F.

or

Helene Fischer
for
Anthony Pratt

When a private secretary actually composes a letter for her employer, she signs as follows:

Yours very truly,

Helene Fischer

Secretary to Mr. Pratt

10. Identification or Reference Data

a. Identification initials are usually placed below the typed signature and flush with the left margin. If the name of the writer does not appear on the page, either in printed or typewritten form, the name of the writer should be typed at the left margin, six spaces below the complimentary close. The initials of the typist should follow the name or initials of the dictator, either in small letters or solid caps. If the name of the dictator is typed in the closing section, it is not necessary to type his initials at the left, but the typist's initials are always shown. No particular style is required for reference initials, unless one is stipulated in a particular office. Following are some samples of reference initials:

FRP:bh	FRPratt:bh	
bh	FRPratt/BH	
FRP:BH	FRP:26	(If a number has been assigned to a typist.)
FRP/bh		

Occasionally in business or professional work, one person may dictate a letter for a person who is in a higher rank and will sign the name of the higher-ranking person. In such case the reference initials would be:

HGM:FRP:bh
HGM/FRP:bh *or*
HGM-FRP:bh

b. Enclosure notations should be written one or two spaces below the reference initials. The number or kind of enclosures may also be specified:

Enclosure
Enclosures 3
Enclosure: Form 554

Other notations may follow the reference initials, such as:

Brochure mailed separately

c. Copy Notations

When several copies of a letter are necessary, reference to each recipient should be noted. The names are arranged in order of importance. When the people are of equal importance, or if the rank is not known, the names should be arranged in alphabetical order. In each case, the proper title should be indicated:

Copy to: Gerard Clyne, M.D.
John McGuire, Ph.D.
Mr. Frank Smith

A copy of the letter may be sent to a person without the knowledge of other addressees. In such case it is considered to be a "blind" copy, and notation should be made accordingly:

bc: Edward M. Reade, Esq.

While the blind copy does not appear on the original, it must appear on the office copy as well as on the copy being sent to the particular party.

Formerly, the letters "cc" were used to denote carbon copy. With the common use of copying machines, the copy really is not a carbon copy; consequently, the prevailing form is "Copy to", or "bc" denoting a blind copy.

d. Postscripts

Postscripts are used either for emphasis or for afterthoughts. They may or may not be preceded by the letters *P. S.* The postscript is either indented or in block form, according to the format of the letter.

C. ILLUSTRATIVE FORMS FOR BUSINESS LETTERS

The letters illustrated on the following pages contain examples of current styles of business letters, punctuation, special features of letters and envelopes.

1. Punctuation Styles

In modern business practice in the United States, no punctuation mark is placed at the end of the lines in an inside address. A few firms, however, have carried over the practice of "closed" punctuation from the earlier years. Some foreign correspondents also use punctuation at the end of the lines of an address. The indented form of an address is rarely used at the present time. Practically all business letters are typed with the inside address in block form, whether the body of the letter has indented paragraphs or block paragraphs. Again, these details are matters of preference, and letters should be typed according to the format required by the business firm.

a. *Open* punctuation means that there is no punctuation mark after the salutation or the complimentary close.

b. *Mixed* punctuation means that a mark of punctuation is placed after the salutation and the complimentary close, but not after the addressee's name in a letter.

c. *Closed* punctuation means that punctuation marks are placed at the end of each line of an address, as well as after the salutation and complimentary close.

2. Special Features—Styles of Letters

The four basic types of letters in use at the present time are listed below. The letters are presented in order of simplicity in typing, beginning with the *simplified block style* having neither salutation nor complimentary close, which letter is used principally in advertising. The *full-block style* is streamlined and saves time in typewriting because the tabulator key is not necessary in typing the parts of the letter. In the *modified block style with block paragraphs*, only the date and the complimentary close are indented, usually starting at the vertical center of the page. The *modified block style with indented paragraphs* requires more tabulation; it is a popular style with businessmen particularly for the use of subparagraphs and the indentation or centering of subject matter or special reference material. In addition to the four basic styles which are presented first, the following pages contain six additional letters, each illustrating special features pertinent to business letters.

Letter Number	*Style or Features*
1	AMS Simplified Style (American Management Society)
2	Full Block; Open Punctuation

3	Modified Block; Block Paragraphs; Mixed Punctuation; Tabulation
4	Modified Block; Indented Paragraphs; Mixed Punctuation; Attention Line; Reference Line; Company Name Included in Signature Section; Copy Notation; Enclosure Notation
5	Modified Block; Open Punctuation; Block Paragraphs; Identifying Initials; Enclosure Notation; Mailing Notation; Postscript
6	Inverted Paragraph Style; Open Punctuation; Reference Initials; Enclosure Notation; Subject Matter Notation
7	Official Letter; Modified Block; Indented Paragraphs; Mixed Punctuation; Inside Address at Bottom of Letter
8	Personal Letter; Return Address; Indented Paragraphs; Mixed Punctuation; Name of Addressee at Lower Left-Hand Corner of Letter; No Name Typed in Signature Section
9	Interoffice Memorandum; Block Paragraphs; Attachment Notation
10 (a)	Two-Page Letter: Modified Block Style; Indented Paragraphs; Mixed Punctuation; Subparagraphs
(b)	Second Page of Letter with Two-Line Second-Page Heading and Enclosure Notation

[LETTERHEAD]

January 5, 19—

Wagner Parks Publishing Co. Inc.
672 Chestnut Street
Marietta, Ohio 45750

ROYALTY AND COPYRIGHT REQUIREMENTS

In order to protect the rights of the artists and/or the heirs and estates of the artists which belong to our clients, please furnish us with the following information to enable us to determine royalty fees due:

1. The size of the pages upon which publication will appear.
2. The percentage of a page each reproduction will occupy.
3. Whether the reproduction will be in color or in black and white.

It is imperative that the name of the artist, the title of the work, and the copyright appear at some point in your publication. The copyright for the reproductions may appear at the bottom of each reproduction, at the beginning or end of the publication, or in a list of illustrations.

After printing has been completed, one proof copy of the publication should be sent to this office, indicating the number of copies which have been printed.

Please be advised that all of the foregoing conditions must be fulfilled or the work(s) reproduced will be considered as nonauthorized.

MARCUS POLO - PUBLICATIONS COUNSEL

ur

AMS Simplified Style

Letter No. 1

[LETTERHEAD]

December 15, 19—

Shareholders
Victoria Terrace
Oxford, Maryland 21654

Gentlemen

Having received numerous letters requesting information on the simultaneous issuance of Real Property Demand Notes and the application of payments made thereto, we are obliged to issue this explanatory letter in an effort to clarify the matter.

The tax, by law, is always billed on or before October 15th each year in respect of the succeeding year and becomes due January 1st of the respective year unless you elect to pay quarterly. If you elect to pay quarterly, the first payment must be made on or before January 1st of the respective year.

Whereas many of you elected to pay quarterly on both current tax and prior-year tax statements, but did not clearly indicate the intent to service both statements, your quarterly installments could have inadvertently been posted in total to either the current or prior year balance. If the total quarterly payments were posted to your current balance, you would have been issued a Notice of Arrears requesting full payment of your prior year balance.

If you are satisfied that your quarterly remittance covered your taxes due, please disregard the Notice of Arrears. If you continue to make timely payments throughout the year, the matter should resolve itself. If the balances remain unsettled through December 31st of the current year, your account will attract a 10 percent surcharge.

Respectfully yours

W. J. Sawyer
Acting Treasurer

Full Block; Open Punctuation

Letter No. 2

[LETTERHEAD]

October 10, 19—

Mr. & Mrs. Frank Lewis
2209 East 42nd Street
New York, New York 10017

Dear Mr. & Mrs. Lewis:

You are hereby informed that taxes are now due, owing and unpaid in the sum of $7,544.59, as follows:

Tax Period Ended	*Date of Assessment*	*Unpaid Balance*	*Statutory Additions*	*Total*
12-31-75	4-10-76	$162.47	$ 25.72	$ 188.89
3-31-76	1-31-77	388.07	71.69	459.76
6-30-76	1-31-77	923.34	175.98	1,099.32
9-30-76	1-31-77	694.38	127.94	822.32
9-30-77	8-19-78	929.26	18.95	948.21
12-31-77	8-26-78	982.74	20.11	1,002.85
3-31-78	8-26-78	899.11	18.83	917.74
		TOTAL AMOUNT DUE		$7,544.59

You are hereby notified that all property, rights to property, moneys, credits, and bank deposits now in your possession and belonging to you (or with respect to which you are obligated) and all sums of money or other obligations owing from you, or on which there is a lien provided under Chapter 108, Code of 1970, are hereby levied upon and seized for satisfaction of the aforesaid tax, together with all additions provided by law, and demand is hereby made upon you for the amount necessary to satisfy the liability set forth herein, or for such lesser sum as you may be indebted, to be applied as a payment on your tax liability. Checks or money orders should be made payable to the undersigned.

Yours very truly,

CITY TAX COLLECTOR

Treasurer

Modified Block; Block Paragraphs; Mixed Punctuation; Tabulation

Letter No. 3

[LETTERHEAD]

February 10, 19—

Robinson and Harper, Esqs.
76 Bank Street
Philadelphia, PA 19107

Attention: Alvin Smith, Esq.

Gentlemen:

Re: Apartment 60-C
920 Fifth Avenue

Enclosed are stock power and assignment of lease to be executed by you on behalf of the Estate of Edward I. Robertson. I have conferred with Mr. Pennalt who has approved your execution of these instruments.

Please forward the documents to Mrs. Robertson for her signature as executrix, who will then return them to us.

Although the sale has not been finally approved by the Board of Managers, it appears likely that it will be approved. We are obtaining your signatures on these documents now to facilitate the closing when the sale is approved.

Very truly yours,

PARKVIEW APARTMENTS

President

DJC:mr
Enclosures

Copy to: Mrs. Jack Robertson
Everett Pennalt, Esq.

Modified Block Style; Indented Paragraphs; Mixed Punctuation; Attention Line; Reference Line; Company Name Included in Signature Section; Copy Notation; Enclosure Notation

Letter No. 4

[LETTERHEAD]

(DATE)

CERTIFIED MAIL
RETURN RECEIPT REQUESTED

Mr. Robert A. Manning
Writers Association
4608 Park Place
Cincinnati, Ohio 44702

Dear Mr. Manning

Enclosed herewith are two copies of the proposed stipulation, one of which I have marked up. I would appreciate it if you would give the stipulation some thought and let me know how it can be modified in order for us not to appear prejudiced.

In the first place, I want to make sure that we are not conceding the fact that associate producers receive the differential even though they did no editing of correspondent's copy. In the second place, I want to make certain that we distinguish the work of the radio group from the television group.

Again, please let me know if you see any discrepancies. It would be perfectly permissible for us to add another stipulation to these if that is the only way we can avoid ambiguity and fully protect ourselves.

As you know, the hearing is now set for June 25th, so I would like to attempt to get this stipulation finalized before the hearing date.

Sincerely yours

Mark B. Black

rnu
Enclosures

P. S. I am also enclosing the transcript for the short hearing on May 30th, together with the bill for it, which I would like to see paid.

Modified Block Style; Open Punctuation; Block Paragraphs; Identifying Initials; Enclosure Notation; Mailing Notation; Postscript. (Note: The letters P. S. may be omitted before the postscript.)

Letter No. 5

[LETTERHEAD]

(DATE)

Messrs. Adams and Kendall
386 East 124 Street
Euclid, Ohio 44123

Re: $750,000 First Mortgage
Loan to Property Investors
Covering Premises in
Tennessee Heights

Gentlemen

In connection with the above captioned mortgage, we enclose herewith the following documents:

Liability —Insurance Company Policy No. 6661 50 90
1. Endorsement adding Property Investors and Savings Bank as additional insureds.
2. Mortgage Clause to Savings Bank

Umbrella —Casualty Company Policy No. QCT 703 81 76
1. Endorsement adding Property Investors and Savings Bank as additional insureds.
2. Mortgage Clause to Savings Bank.

Fire —Insurance Association Policy No. 207200006
1. Certificate of Insurance issued to Savings Bank.

We anticipate receiving this week the endorsement adding an additional insured under the fire policy and the loss payable clause. Upon receipt thereof, I will immediately transmit same to you.

We thank you for your cooperation in this matter.

Very truly yours

Secretary-Treasurer

RFG:et
Enclosures

Inverted Paragraph Style; Open Punctuation; Reference Initials; Enclosure Notation; Subject Matter Notation.

Letter No. 6

[LETTERHEAD]

(DATE)

Dear Stephen:

After your telephone call, I spoke with Frank Gilbert, and he would be interested in developing a plan for your financing purposes. His connections in the banking field are significant.

Your documentary was very well balanced in terms of its analysis of the problem, the photography was excellently done and edited, and the overall impact of the program was quite dramatic. For the most part, your on-camera people choices were excellent.

I am pleased to advise you that several days ago, through the National Bank, we were able to arrange for the transfer of all of the stock that was still held in your father's estate. I will advise you when the entire transfer has been made.

Sincerely,

Lee M. Clifford

Mr. Stephen Moore
One Sherwood Parkway
Westbrook, New Jersey 07762

LMC:bh

Official Letter; Modified Block Style; Indented Paragraphs; Mixed Punctuation; Inside Address at Bottom of Letter.

Letter No. 7

1690 Sycamore Road
Cleveland, Ohio 44120
August 25, 19—

Dear Brian,

It's been a long time since we have been in touch. I still regret that I did not get down to Kenya last fall, and I am planning now to arrange to get out that way sometime this year.

One of my hopes is to be able to get away to attend the Legal Foundation program on private international transactions in Africa, which I understand is scheduled to be held in Ethiopia in October. It is possible that I may get there earlier, but nothing is definite at this juncture.

I am very interested in learning of the implications to your operations of the decree which was promulgated in late December, establishing new rules governing the activities of foreigners in selected fields, including law practice.

Last week I met a friend of yours, Timothy Quinn, who apparently is quite knowledgeable in regard to foreign legal transactions. I was quite impressed with Tim and I hope there will be opportunities for us to collaborate professionally with him.

I would be interested in learning how matters are progressing in your area. If you have a spare moment, do drop me a line.

Best regards.

Cordially,

Mr. Brian Burke
P. O. Box 1895
Bangkok, THAILAND

Personal Letter; Return Address; Indented Paragraphs; Mixed Punctuation; Name of Addressee at Lower Left-Hand Corner of Letter; No Name Typed in Signature Section.

Letter No. 8

[HEADING]

TO	All Residents
FROM	The Management (Peter Mohr)
DATE	June 30, 19—
SUBJECT	Disposal of Rubbish

Many of the tenants have been complaining about the disposal of rubbish in the compactor chute.

The incinerators were replaced with compactors to eliminate soot, smoke, and odors. Many tenants have been leaving garbage in the service hall instead of placing this garbage into the chute.

Please direct your maids to follow these rules in order to help the building personnel keep the area clean:

1. Place all garbage in small paper or plastic bags that will fit into the chute.
2. Coathangers, large boxes or metal rods should be left in the compactor room.
3. Newspapers should be placed in the special receptacle which we have placed in each service hall.

If you have any questions concerning these matters, please telephone the Manager.

P. M.

PM:wd
Attachment

Interoffice Memorandum; Block Paragraphs; Attachment Notation.

Letter No. 9

[LETTERHEAD]

September 10, 19—

Peterson & Company
104 East 38 Street
New York, New York 10016

Gentlemen:

Re: Jones Electronics Corporation

In connection with your regular examination of the accounts of the above company as at June 30, 19—, we advise you of the following:

1. We know of no unsettled judgments, litigation of claims for damages, patent infringement claims, etc., against the company.

2. We know of no pending actions arising from alleged violations of laws or regulations relating to securities (registration, trading, etc.) wages, trade, etc.

3. We know of no commitments of the company to purchase any of its own stock, the stock or assets of another company, or any other securities or business interests, including related provisions of stockholders' agreements.

4. We know of no other major commitments not in the ordinary course of business, such as the purchase or construction of real estate or other items of substantial amount.

5. We know of no existing subordination of debt by stockholders, officers, or other creditors.

6. We know of no guarantee of company debt by stockholders, officers, or others.

7. We know of no accommodation notes or acceptances, or endorsements of guarantees or obligations of others by the company.

Two-Page Letter: Modified Block Style, Indented Paragraphs, Mixed Punctuation; Subparagraphs

Letter No. 10

Peterson & Company | September 10, 19—
Page 2

We further advise you that we know of no contracts or agreements in the process of negotiation or renegotiation, nor are we holding any accounts for collection. So far as we know, no leases have been signed during the past twelve months.

At the present time there are no unpaid charges for services or expenses due us.

To our knowledge, there is no other matter, whether pending or already settled, representing any actual or contingent present or future liability, which may affect the company's financial position.

We trust the above information is satisfactory for your purposes.

Yours very truly,

WEBER and WEISS

By ______________________
Partner

MG:rs

Enclosure

Second Page of Letter with Two-Line Second-Page Heading and Enclosure Notation

[redacted]

REGISTERED MAIL

Attention: Kenneth Fleming, Esq.
Patent Counsel

The Gold Fibre Company
2670 Hamilton Place
Allentown, Pennsylvania 07424

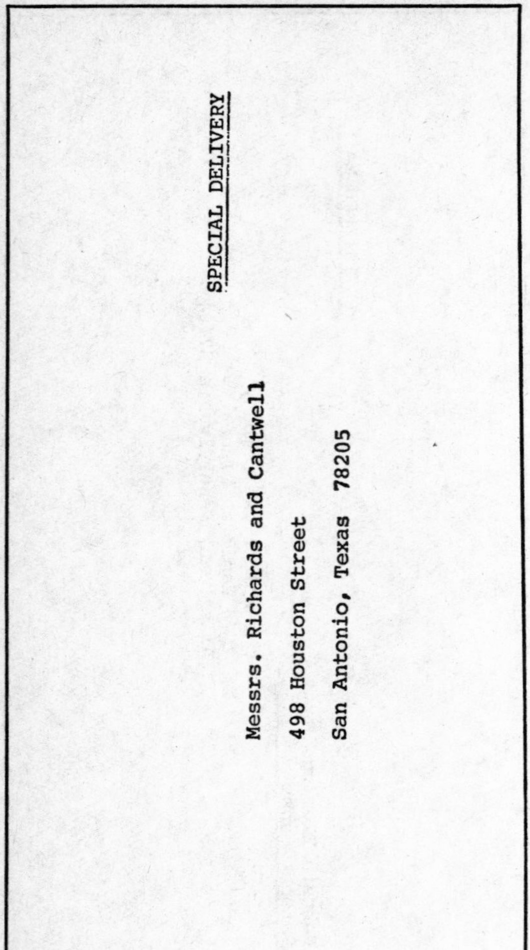
SPECIAL DELIVERY
Messrs. Richards and Cantwell
498 Houston Street
San Antonio, Texas 78205

[redacted]

CERTIFIED MAIL
RETURN RECEIPT REQUESTED

Dr. Matthew Kielty

460 Washington Avenue

Chicago, Illinois 60602

[redacted]

BY HAND

Professor Theodore Stiles
1740 McBride Avenue
Little Falls, NJ 07424

PERSONAL AND
CONFIDENTIAL
Mr. Brian Burke
P. O. Box 1895
Bangkok
THAILAND

HOLD FOR ARRIVAL

Harold Stanley, M. D.
Imperial Hotel
100 Gulf Road
Olympia, Washington 98504

Chapter 9

FORMS OF ADDRESS AND SALUTATION—DOMESTIC AND FOREIGN

The inside address in a business letter must contain the title of the person to whom the letter is addressed. The envelope should contain the corresponding information. Titles are words of courtesy, and care must be exercised that the correct title is used. The salutation of a letter is a reflection of the title, and the complimentary close is influenced by the salutation. No office worker can be expected to know offhand every title and salutation to use, but he should know that there are reference books available containing such information, for example, manuals or reference material in the library, and dictionaries in the office. A useful reference book for the office is the United States Office Style Manual, Superintendent of Documents, Washington, D. C.

This chapter presents the most common forms of address called for in business correspondence. The forms of address and complimentary close of letters vary according to the relationship between the correspondents. Therefore no definite forms can be given for all situations. While the lists included here are not entirely comprehensive, an attempt is made to present proper forms of addresses for certain officials and dignitaries, both domestic and foreign, on the local, state and national levels, for military personnel, and for clergy of various religious denominations.

A. TITLES OF INDIVIDUALS AND BUSINESS AFFILIATIONS

1. Individuals

Explanation	*Individual*	*Salutation*
Man	Mr. Vincent Weissman	Dear Mr. Weissman Dear Sir Dear Vincent
Married Woman or Widow	Mrs. William Bennett or Mrs. Alice Bennett	Dear Mrs. Bennett Dear Madam Dear Alice
Divorced Woman	(if she retains her husband's surname) Mrs. Alice Bennett (a divorced woman does not use her husband's first name)	Dear Mrs. Bennett Dear Madam Dear Alice
Man and Wife	Mr. and Mrs. David Fischer Dr. and Mrs. Basil Fischer	Dear Mr. and Mrs. Fischer Dear Dr. and Mrs. Fischer
Unmarried Woman	Miss Lucille Briggs	Dear Miss Briggs Dear Madam My dear Miss Briggs

Marital Status Unknown	Ms. Florence Kennedy	Dear Ms. Kennedy
Two or more Unmarried Women	The Misses Belknap *or* Misses Fran and Flo Belknap	Dear Misses Belknap Ladies
Two or more Married Women	Mmes. Brown and Ward	Ladies Mesdames
Boy under 13 years of age	Master Edward Smith	Dear Edward Dear Master Smith
Two Brothers	Messrs. Edward and James Smith	Dear Sirs

2. Business Affiliations

Partnership	Messrs. Brown and Smith	Gentlemen Dear Sirs
Partnership with Attention	Messrs. Brown and Smith Attention: Mr. Paul Smith	Gentlemen Dear Sirs *Dear Mr. Smith
Attorney	Mark Murray, Esq.	Dear Mr. Murray Dear Sir
Law Firms	Block and White, Esqs. Fried Smith Jones, Esqs.	Gentlemen Dear Sirs

Explanation	*Names*	*Salutation*
Name of Firm with Attention	Fried Smith Jones, Esqs. Attention: Abe Smith, Esq.	Gentlemen Dear Sirs *Dear Mr. Smith
Attorney with Firm	Bernard Jones, Esq. Messrs. Fried Smith Jones	Dear Mr. Jones Dear Sir
Name of Firm Attention of Woman Attorney	Fried Smith Jones, Esqs. Attention: Mary Quinn, Esq.	Gentlemen Dear Sirs *Dear Ms. Quinn
Woman Attorney with Firm	Mary Quinn, Esq. Messrs. Fried Smith Jones	Dear Ms. (Miss or Mrs.) Quinn
Corporate Executive	Mr. Robert Reade Vice President Atlas Corporation	Dear Mr. Reade Dear Sir
Corporation Attention of Executive	Atlas Corporation Attention: Mr. Robert Reade Vice President	Gentlemen Dear Sirs *Dear Mr. Reade
Corporate Woman Executive	Miriam Gorham, Esq. General Counsel Atlas Corporation	Dear (Ms., Mrs., or Miss) Gorham
Corporation Attention of Woman Executive	Atlas Corporation Attention Miriam Gorham, Esq. General Counsel	Gentlemen Dear Sirs *Dear (Ms., Mrs., or Miss) Gorham

*Note: Some authorities hold that it is improper to address the individual in the salutation when the firm is named first. It is common practice, however, to direct the salutation to the person whose name is mentioned in the Attention line.

B. TITLES OF GOVERNMENT OFFICIALS

Official	*Address*	*Salutation*
President of the United States	The President The White House Washington, D. C. 20500	Sir Mr. President Dear Mr. President My dear Mr. President
	The Honorable (full name) President of the United States The White House Washington, D. C. 20500	Dear President (surname) My dear President (surname)
The Wife of the President	Mrs. (full name) The White House Washington, D. C. 20500	Dear Mrs. (surname) My dear Mrs. (surname)
Vice President of the United States	The Vice President *or* The Vice President of the United States *or* The Honorable (full name) Vice President of the United States	Sir My dear Sir Dear Sir Mr. Vice President My dear Vice President (surname) Dear Vice President (surname)
	United States Senate Washington, D. C. 20510	

Official	*Address*	*Salutation*
Chief Justice of the United states	The Chief Justice *or* The Chief Justice of the United States The Supreme Court Washington, D. C. 20543 *or* The Honorable (full name) Chief Justice of the Supreme Court of the United States Washington, D. C. 20543	Sir Mr. Chief Justice Dear Mr. Chief Justice My dear Mr. Chief Justice
Associate Justice of the Supreme Court	Mr. Justice (full name) The Supreme Court of the United States Washington, D. C. 20543 *or* The Honorable (full name) Associate Justice of the Supreme Court Washington, D. C. 20543	Sir Mr. Justice My dear Mr. Justice My dear Justice (surname) Dear Justice (surname)
Speaker of the House of Representatives	The Honorable (full name) Speaker of the House of Representatives Washington, D. C. 20515 *or*	Sir My dear Sir Mr. Speaker My dear Mr. Speaker

	The Speaker of the House Representatives Washington, D. C. 20515	My dear Mr. (surname) Dear Mr. (surname)
Cabinet Member	The Secretary of ______ Washington, D. C. 20502 *or* The Honorable (full name) Secretary of ______ Washington, D. C. 20502	Sir My dear Sir Dear Sir My dear Mr. Secretary Dear Mr. Secretary
Secretary to the President	The Honorable (full name) Secretary to the President The White House Washington, D. C. 20500	Dear Mr. (surname)
Secretary to the President President with military rank	(name and full rank) Secretary to the President The White House Washington, D. C. 20500	Sir Dear (rank)
Senator (Male)	The Honorable (full name) The United States Senate Washington, D. C. 20510 *or* Senator (full name) The United States Senate Washington, D. C. 20510 (or local address)	Sir My dear Sir Dear Sir My dear Mr. Senator My dear Senator Dear Senator Dear Senator (surname) My dear Senator (surname)

Official	*Address*	*Salutation*
Senator (Female)	The Honorable (full name) The United States Senate Washington, D. C. 20510 *or* Senator (full name) The United States Senate Washington, D. C. 20510 (or local address)	Madam Dear Madam My dear Senator (surname) My dear Madam Senator Dear (Mrs., Ms., or Miss) (surname)
Representative (Male)	The Honorable (full name) The House of Representatives Washington, D. C. 20515 Representative (full name) The House of Representatives Washington, D. C. 20515	Dear Representative (surname) Dear Mr. (surname) Sir My dear Sir Dear Sir My dear Congressman
Representative (Female)	The Honorable (full name) The House of Representatives Washington, D. C. 20515 Representative (full name) The House of Representatives Washington, D. C. 20515	Madam Dear Madam Dear Mrs. (surname) My dear Mrs. (surname) Dear Representative (surname)

Governor of a State	The Honorable (full name) Governor of (State) (City and State + zip code) (*or* in some States) His Excellency The Governor of (State) City, State	Sir Dear Sir My dear Sir Dear Governor (surname) My dear Governor (surname)
State Senator (Male)	The Honorable (full name) The State Senate City, State, zip code	Sir My dear Sir Dear Sir Dear Mr. Senator Dear Senator (surname)
State Senator (Female)	The Honorable (full name) The State Senate City, State, zip code	Madam Dear Madam Dear Senator (surname) My dear Senator (surname)
State Assemblyman	The Honorable (full name) Member of the Assembly The State Capitol City, State, zip code Assemblyman (or State Representative) (surname) The State Capitol City, State, zip code	Sir My dear Sir Dear Mr. (surname) My dear Mr. (surname)

Official	*Address*	*Salutation*
State Representative (Female)	The Honorable (full name) Member of the Assembly The State Capitol City, State, zip code *or* State Representative (surname)	Dear Madam Dear (Mrs., Ms., or Miss) (surname) My dear (Mrs., Ms., or Miss) (surname)
Mayor (Male)	The Honorable (full name) Mayor of ________ (*or*) Mayor of the City of ________ City Hall City, State, zip code	Dear Mr. Mayor My dear Mr. Mayor Sir Dear Sir Dear Mayor (surname)
(Female)	The Honorable (full name) Mayor of ________ (*or*) Mayor of the City of ________ City Hall City, State, zip code	Dear Madam Madam Dear Mayor (surname) My dear Mayor (surname)
President of Board of Commissioners	The Honorable (full name) President, Board of Commissioners of the city of (name) State and zip code	Sir My dear Mr. (surname)
District Attorney	The Honorable (full name) District Attorney (name) County Local Address	Dear Sir Dear Mr. (surname)

City or Town Council Member	The Honorable (full name) Member of the (City or Town) Council Municipal Building City, State, zip code	Dear Sir Dear Madam Dear Mr. (surname) Dear (Mrs., Ms., Miss) (surname)
Alderman	Alderman (full name) City Hall City, State, zip code	Dear Sir Dear Mr. (surname)
Judge of a Court	The Honorable (full name) Judge of the (name) Court City, State, zip code	Sir Dear Judge (name) My dear Judge (name)
Clerk of a court	(full name), Esq. Clerk of the (name) Court City, State, zip code	Dear Sir Dear Mr. (surname)

Note: In writing to dignitaries and officials, any one of the following complimentary closings is appropriate:

Yours very truly
Very truly yours
Sincerely
Sincerely yours
Yours sincerely
Respectfully
Respectfully yours
Yours respectfully

C. MILITARY OFFICERS AND PERSONNEL

1. Army

Officer	*Address*	*Salutation*
General of the Army	(full name), U.S.A. General of the Army Department of the Army Washington, D. C.	Sir My dear General (surname)
General—Lieutenant, Major, or Brigadier General	General (Lieutenant General, Major General, or Brigadier General) (full name), U.S.A. (Local Address)	Sir My dear General (surname) My dear Lieutenant General (surname) (etc.)
Colonel, Lieutenant Colonel	Colonel (Lieutenant Colonel) (full name), U.S.A. (Local Address)	My dear Colonel (surname) My dear Lieutenant Colonel (surname)
Major	Major (full name), U.S.A. (Local Address)	My dear Major (surname)
Captain	Captain (full name), U.S.A. (Local Address)	My dear Captain (surname)
First Lieutenant, Second Lieutenant	Lieutenant (full name), U.S.A. (Local Address)	My dear Lieutenant (surname)
Chaplain in the United States Army	Chaplain (full name) Captain, U.S.A. (Local Address)	My dear Chaplain My dear Chaplain (surname)

Noncommissioned Officers	Title and Name Serial Number Station Service Address (City, State, Country)	Dear (title & surname) Dear Sir My dear Sir Dear Madam Dear Mr., Mrs., Ms., or Miss (surname)

Note: Air Force titles and Marine Corps titles are the same as those of the Army, except that the top rank in the Marine Corps is "Commandant of the Marine Corps". The initials U.S.A.F. are used for the Air Force, and U.S.M.C. are used for the Marine Corps.
Reserves are denoted as follows: U.S.M.R. (Marine Corps). U.S.A. is changed to A.U.S. (Army of the United States) for the Army, and to A.F.U.S. for the Air Force

2. Navy

U.S.N. indicates regular service.
U.S.N.R. denotes the Reserve.

Officer	*Address*	*Salutation*
Admiral	Admiral (full name), U.S.N. Chief of Naval Operations Department of the Navy Washington, D. C.	Sir My dear Admiral (surname)
Fleet Admiral	Fleet Admiral (full name), U.S.N. (Address)	Sir My dear Admiral (surname)
Rear Admiral	Rear Admiral (full name), U.S.N (Address)	Sir My dear Admiral (surname)
Vice Admiral	Vice Admiral (full name), U.S.N. (Address)	Sir My dear Admiral (surname)

Officer	*Address*	*Salutation*
Commodore, Captain, Commander	Commodore (full name), U.S.N. (Address)	My dear Commodore (Captain, Commander) Dear Commodore (Captain, Commander) (surname)
Lieutenant Commander, Lieutenant, Lieutenant Junior Grade Ensign	Lieutenant Commander (Lieutenant, Lieutenant Junior Grade, Ensign) (full name), U.S.N. (Address)	Dear Mr. (surname) My dear (surname) Dear (Lieutenant Commander, Lieutenant, Ensign) (surname)
Chaplain*	Captain (full name), (Ch.C.), U.S.N. Department of the Navy Washington, D. C.	Reverend Sir My dear Chaplain Dear Chaplain (surname)

*Roman Catholic chaplains and certain Anglican chaplains are referred to as "Father (name)" but are introduced as "Chaplain (name)"

Note: All officers, whether commissioned or noncommissioned, should be addressed by their titles. Other members of the services should have the name prefixed by the rank, such as, Sgt. (full name) Pfc. (full name). The OFFICIAL REGISTER of the armed services provides current listings of divisions and classifications.

D. PROFESSIONAL TITLES

Name and Title	*Explanation*	*Salutation*
1. Medical Profession		
Dr. (full name) *or* (full name), M.D. (full name), D.D.S. *Incorrect* Dr. Mark Wayne, M.D.	It is preferable to have the degree designation follow the name. When a professional degree is used after a name, no title should appear before the name.	Dear Dr. (surname) My dear Dr. (surname) Dear Sir Dear Doctor My dear Sir My dear Doctor
2. Legal Profession		
(full name), Esq. (for men and women) *or* (full name), J.D. Carl Rogers, Esq. Messrs. Hart, Rogers, Brown and Dunne Hart, Rogers, Brown and Dunne, Esqs. Attention: Carl Rogers, Esq.	J.D. stands for Juris Doctor and is the present title of the first law degree, formerly designated as the LL.B. degree. The second degree is the Master of Law. The "J.D." is rarely used in a title. The abbreviation "Esq." is preferred.	Dear Sir My dear Sir Dear Madam My dear Madam Dear Mr. (surname) My dear Mr. (surname) Dear (Ms., Ms., or Miss) (surname)

Name and Title	*Explanation*	*Salutation*
3. University of College Professors		
President (full name) Name of College or University *or* (full name) (degree initials) President Name of College or University	University or College President (When writing to a Dean, substitute the word "Dean" for "President")	Dear President (surname) My dear President (surname)
Faculty (full name) Ph.D. (full name)) Ed.D. (full name) D.B.A. (full name) Litt.D.	The title "Dr." is used with the name of any person having a degree containing the letter "D": M.D., D.D.S., J.D., Ph.D., Ed.D., D.B.A., LL.D., Litt.D., L.H.D., etc.	Dear Sir Dear Madam Dear Dr. (surname) My dear Dr. (surname)
Prof. Grace Byrne, Ph.D. Name of College or University	It is permissible to use two professional titles for one person if each title has a different connotation.	Dear Prof. (surname) Dear Professor (surname) Dear Dr. (surname) My dear Dr. (surname)

E. RELIGIOUS TITLES

Dignitary	*Address*	*Salutation*
1. Jewish Faith		
Rabbi	Rabbi (full name)	Dear Rabbi (surname) Dear Rabbi Dear Dr. (surname)
2. Protestant Episcopal		
Bishop	The Right Reverend (full name) Bishop of (diocese) *or* The Right Reverend John Smith, D.D., LL.D. Bishop of (place)	Right Reverend Sir Dear Bishop (surname)
Dean	Dean (full name) *or* The Very Reverend (full name)	Very Reverend Sir Dear Dean (surname)
3. Protestant Bishop (other than Episcopal)		
Bishop	The Reverend (full name), D.D. Methodist Bishop (local address)	Reverend Sir Dear Bishop Dear Bishop (surname)
4. Protestant Clergymen		
Clergyman	The Reverend (full name) *or* Reverend Dr. (full name) *or* Reverend (full name), D.D.	Dear Sir Dear Mr. (surname) Dear Dr. (surname)

5. Roman Catholic Church

Dignitary	*Salutation*	*Complimentary Close*
a. The Pope		
His Holiness Pope (NAME) *or* His Holiness the Pope	Your Holiness *or* Most Holy Father	Your dutiful (son or daughter) *or* Respectfully yours
b. Cardinal		
His Eminence (first name) Cardinal (surname) Archbishop of (Diocese) (Street Address)	Your Eminence Dear Cardinal (surname)	Respectfully yours

c. Dignitaries and Clergy

Dignitary	*Address*	*Salutation*
Archbishop	The Most Reverend Archbishop of (diocese) *or* The Most Reverend (full name) S.T.D. Archbishop of (diocese)	Your Excellency Dear Archbishop (surname)
Bishop	The Most Reverend (full name) S.T.D. Bishop of (diocese) (local address)	Your Excellency Dear Bishop (surname)

Monsignor	The Very Reverend Monsignor (full name) (local address)	Dear Monisgnor (surname)
Priest	The Reverend Father (surname) *or* Rev. (full name)	Dear Father (surname) Dear Reverend Father
d. Members of Religious Institutions		
(1) *Superior of a Brotherhood (Roman Catholic)*		
	Brother (name) (F.S.C. or other initials of order) Superior (Name of Institution) (Local Address)	Dear Brother (first name) *or* Dear Brother (surname)
(2) *Superior of a Brotherhood (Protestant)*		
	(full name) (religious intitials) Superior (Name of Institution) (Local Address)	Dear Brother (first name) *or* Dear Brother (surname)
(3) *Superior of a Sisterhood*		
	Reverend Mother (first name or surname, as desired) (initials of order) *or* The Reverend Mother Superior	Reverend Mother Reverend Mother (name) Dear Reverend Mother

Dignitary	*Address*	*Salutation*
(4) *Member of a Sisterhood*		
	Sister (name) (initials of order) *or* Sister (name) (order spelled out)	Dear Sister Dear Sister (name)

F. UNITED NATIONS REPRESENTATIVES

The title of a representative to the United Nations is determined either by the position he holds in his Government's service and/or by the nature of his position at the United Nations.

Official	*Address*	*Salutation*
Secretary General	His Excellency (full name) Secretary General of the United Nations United Nations, New York 10017	Excellency Dear Mr. Secretary General Dear Mr. (surname)
Assistant Secretary General	The Honorable (full name) Assistant Secretary General of the United Nations United Nations, New York 10017	Sir Dear Sir Dear Mr. (surname)

Foreign Representative to U. N. with rank of Ambassador	His Excellency (full name) Representative of (country) to the United Nations (Address)	Excellency Dear Mr. Ambassador Dear Ambassador (surname) Dear Sir
United States Representative to the U. N.	The Honorable (full name) United States Representative to the United Nations New York, New York 10017	Sir Dear Sir Dear Mr. (surname)
Senior Representative of the United States to the General Assembly	The Honorable (full name) Senior Representative of the United States to the General Assembly of the United Nations	Dear Sir Dear Mr. (surname)
U. S. Representative on the Economic and Social Council	The Honorable (full name) United States Representative on the Economic and Social Council of the United Nations	Dear Sir Dear Mr. (surname)
U. S. Representative on the Trusteeship Council	The Honorable (full name) United States Representative on the Trusteeship Council of the United Nations	Dear Sir Dear Mr. (surname)

Note: The complimentary close in any of the above situations may be:

Very truly yours
Yours very truly
Sincerely yours
Yours sincerely

G. DIPLOMATS

1. United States of America

Personage	*Address*	*Salutation*
American Ambassador (Man or Woman)	The Honorable (full name) American Ambassador (City, Country)	Dear Sir Dear Madam My dear Mr. Ambassador My dear Madam Ambassador
American Minister (Man or Woman)	The Honorable (full name) American Minister (City, Country)	Sir Madam My dear Mr. Minister My dear Madam Minister My dear (Mrs., Ms., Miss) (surname)
American Chargé d'Affaires	(full name), Esq. American Charge d'Affaires (City, Country)	Dear Sir Dear Mr. (surname)
American Consul General, Consul, or Vice Consul	(full name), Esq. American Consul General (or Consul, or Vice Consul) (City, Country)	Dear Sir Dear Mr. (surname) Dear (Mrs., Ms., Miss) (surname)
High Commissioner	The United States High Commissioner to (country) (Address) *or*	Sir Madam My dear Mr. Commissioner My dear Commissioner (surname)

	The Honorable (full name) United States High Commissioner to (country) (Address)	
American Ambassador (with military rank)	(Rank) (full name) American Ambassador	Dear (rank & surname) Sir Dear (rank) Dear Ambassador

2. Foreign Ambassadors in the United States

Ambassador (name known)	His Excellency (full name) Ambassador of (place)	Excellency Sir Dear Sir
(name unknown)	His Excellency The Ambassador of (country or place)	Dear Mr. Ambassador Dear Ambassador (name)
Minister from Foreign Country	The Honorable (full name) Minister of (name of place) *or* Mr. (full name) Minister of (name of place)	Sir Dear Sir Dear Mr. Minister Dear Mr. (surname)
Chargé d'Affaires	Baron (full name) Chargé d'Affaires of (place)	Sir Dear Sir Dear Baron (name)

Personage	*Address*	*Salutation*
Foreign Diplomat with a Personal Title	His Excellency Count (full name) Ambassador of (country)	Excellency My dear Mr. Ambassador
President of a Republic	His Excellency (full name) President of the Republic of the Ivory Coast (Address)	Excellency My dear Mr. President My dear President (surname)

H. CANADIAN OFFICIALS

1. Governor General (with rank)	His excellency (Duke, Earl, Viscount, etc.) Governor General of Canada Ottawa, Canada	Excellency Sir Dear Governor General Dear (title) (surname) Dear Mr. (surname)
(without rank)	His Excellency Governor General of Canada Ottawa, Canada	
2. Prime Minister	Right Honorable (full name with honors, if any) Prime Minister of the Dominion of Canada Ottawa, Canada	Sir Dear Sir Dear Mr. Prime Minister Dear Mr. (surname)

Note: The title of all ambassadors and ministers of foreign countries is "Ambassador of ________"; "Minister of ________", with the exception of Great Britain, which title is "British Ambassador" or "British Minister."

I. BRITISH OFFICIALS

Personage	*Address*	*Salutation*
British Prime Minister	The Right Honorable (full name), M.P. Prime Minister London, England	Sir My dear Mr. Prime Minister My dear Mr. (surname)
Member of the British Cabinet	The Right Honorable (full name), P.C.* Secretary of State for Foreign Affairs London, England	Sir My dear Mr. (surname) My dear Mr. Secretary of State
Lord Chief Justice	The Right Honorable The Lord Chief Justice of England London, England *or* (If he is a peer in his own right, he is addressed by his title of nobility) The Lord Chief Justice of England London, England	Sir My dear Lord Chief Justice

*All members of the British Cabinet are members of the Privy Council and as such are entitled to the intials "P.C." after their names.

Personage	*Address*	*Salutation*
England		
Judge (High Court of Justice)	The Hon. Mr. Justice (surname) The Hon. Sir (full name)	Sir Dear Mr. Justice (surname) Dear Sir (first name)
Judge of County Court	His Honour Judge (full name)	Sir Dear Judge (surname)
Commonwealth		
Knight	Sir (full name)	Sir Dear Sir (full name) Dear Sir (first name)
Knight's wife	Lady (surname)	Madam Dear Lady (surname)
London, York, Belfast, or Dublin		
Lord Mayor	The Rt. Hon. The Lord Mayor of (place)	My Lord My dear Lord Mayor
Lord Mayor's wife	The Rt. Hon. The Lady Mayoress of (place)	Madam My dear Lady Mayoress

J. FOREIGN EXPRESSIONS FOR MR., MRS., MISS

Children: Currently, either no title at all, or the titles of Mr. and Miss are used in letters to children. Formerly, a boy was called "Master" before his teens, and a girl had no title before her teens. This practice is still correct.

Personage	*Address*	*Salutation*
1. French		
Mr. Monsier	Monsieur Pierre L'Amour M. Pierre L'Amour	Monsieur Cher Monsieur Cher Monsieur (surname)
Mrs. Madame	Madame Pierre L'Amour	Madame Chère Madame Chère Madame (surname)
Miss Mademoiselle	Mademoiselle Marie L'Amour	Mademoiselle Chère Mademoiselle Chère Mademoiselle (surname)

Personage	*Address*	*Salutation*
2. German		
Mr. Herrn	Herrn Jon Metz	Sehr geehrter Herr Metz Lieber Herr Metz
Mrs. Frau	Frau Metz	Sehr geehrte Frau Metz Liebe Frau Metz
Miss Fräulein	Fräulein Freda Metz	Sehr geehrtes Fräulein Metz Liebes Fräulein Metz
3. Italian		
Mr. Signor	Signor Ernest Carcone	Gentile Signore My dear Signor Carcone My dear Signore
Mrs. Signora	Signora Maria Carcone	Gentile Signora My dear Signora
Miss Signorina	Signorina Sophia Carcone	Gentile Signorina My dear Signorina
4. Portuguese		
Senior Official (chief officer)	A Sua Excelencia o Senhor (full name)	Senhor Secretary of State (*or*) Senhor Ambassador (*or*) Senhor Admiral Senhor (surname)

Official Person (Consul, Director, etc.)	Ao Senhor (full name)	Senhor Consul (*or*) Senhor Director (*or*) Senhor Commissioner
	A sua Senhoria (full name)	Senhor (surname)
Mr. (without title) Senhor	A Sua Senhor (full name)	Senhor (surname) Prezada Amigo Senhor (surname)
Mrs. Senhora	Senhora Dona Mary (surname)	Excma. Senhora Prezada Senhora Dona Mary
Miss Senhorita	Senhorita Dorita (surname)	Excma. Senhorita Prezada Senhorita Dorita

5. Spanish

Mr. Señor	Señor Don John Jones	Muy Señor mio Distinguido amigo
Mrs. Señora	Sra. Da. Mary Jones de Hernandez Señora de Hernandez	Ilma. Señora Distinguida Señora
Miss Señorita	Señorita Dona Anita Jones Srta. Da. Anita Jones	Distinguida Señorita Señorita Jones Mi distinguida amiga

Note: The complimentary close for foreign correspondents is any of the following:

Yours sincerely
Sincerely yours
Yours very truly
Very truly yours

Chapter 10

ESSENTIAL REFERENCE DATA

This chapter contains reference material which the secretary may frequently have to refer to in the course of her work, and which information is not always readily available in reference books in the office. Of particular significance are features of report writing: where to look for material, how to formulate a sequential outline, pagination of the manuscript, and the correct form for footnotes and bibliography. The format for minutes of both informal and formal business meetings is also included, together with a list of proofreader's marks.

This chapter also presents a list of capitals of the United States, Canadian capitals, and capitals of the world. Additional information is supplied in relation to dimensions of the continents, to Arabic figures and Roman numerals.

Reference is made to the implications of the Metric System, and a summary outline is presented for the basic units and common prefixes of the system. Metric terms, symbols, and equivalents are listed in outline form.

A. REPORT WRITING

Secretaries at times have to type papers for executives who may be called upon to speak at a business conference or a management seminar. A legal secretary frequently has to type a lengthy memorandum of law, and medical secretaries may be asked to type papers for doctors to present at a medical meeting. Such reports usually include footnotes, a bibliography, and sometimes an annotated bibliography. The secretary may even have to go to a public or private library to obtain material supplementary to the reference material in an office. The information presented here should serve as a guide to typing footnotes and a bibliography, and as an aid to the secretary in locating book sections in a library.

1. The Dewey Decimal System of Cataloging

00	General
100	Philosophy
200	Religion
300*	Social Science
400	Language
500	Science and Mathematics
600*	Applied Sciences and Industries
700	Literature
800	History, Travel, and Biography

*Sections 300 and 600 relate to business.

2. Footnotes

In typing footnotes, care should be taken that adequate white space is left at the bottom of the page (at least 1¼" of white space). Type a line (15 spaces) one space below the last line of the text to separate the footnote from the text. Begin the footnote a double space below the typed line and indent the first line of the footnote about five spaces from the left margin; the second and third lines, etc., of the footnote are typed at the margin. While each footnote *per se* is typed single space, a double space is left between each footnote. Use either superior numbers or symbols to identify the footnotes. For example (quoted material):

> . . . Where a lawyer knows of legal authority in the controlling jurisdiction directly adverse to the position of his client, he

should inform the tribunal of its existence unless his adversary has done so; but, having made such disclosure, he may challenge the soundness in whole or in part.*

Note: Some authorities hold that it is not necessary to indicate quoted material with quotation marks, if the material is set off in single space. The fact that it is set off from a double-spaced text and is single spaced is sufficient to indicate that it is quoted material. Such a practice also keeps quoted material intact in double quotation marks as it appears in the original document or text.

3. Bibliography

The bibliography identifies source material and is usually placed at the end of each chapter or at the close of the manuscript. A bibliography is always in hanging indention form and is in alphabetical order, according to author. If the reference has only one author, the surname is placed first. If there are two or more authors, the name of the first author only is transposed; the names of the other authors are given in respective order. Magazine articles or chapters in a book are enclosed in quotation marks, and the name of the publication is underscored. Bibliography styles vary.

BIBLIOGRAPHY

Agnew, Peter L., James R. Meehan, and Mary Ellen Oliverio. Secretarial Office Practice, 7th ed. (Cincinnati, Ohio: South-Western Publishing Co., 1969).

Kerschner, Rachel Guinther. Secretary's Desk Guide to Business English (West Nyack, New York: Parker Publishing Company, Inc., 1977), 239 pp.

Welty, Paul Thomas. "Society in Transition," The Human Expression (New York, N. Y.: J. B. Lippincott Company, 1977), pp. 780-805.

---

*Edward D. Re, *Brief Writing and Oral Arguments*, Fourth Edition (Dobbs Ferry, New York: Oceana Publications, Inc., 1974), pp. 22-3.

4. Paging the Manuscript

Use Arabic numerals for all page numbers in the text. The first page of each chapter is not numbered, but allowance is made for the first page in numbering subsequent pages. Small Roman numerals are used for numbering pages in the index:

Index	*Text*				
i	1		-1-		- 1 -
ii	2		-2-		- 2 -
iii	3		-3-		- 3 -
iv	4		-4-		- 4 -
v	5	*or*	-5-	*or*	- 5 -
vi	6		-6-		- 6 -
vii	7		-7-		- 7 -
viii	8		-8-		- 8 -
ix	9		-9-		- 9 -
x	10		-10-		- 10 -

The above Arabic forms "-5-" "- 5 -" are usually used at the bottom of a page. Some manuscripts are numbered in the upper right-hand corner. In such case, either the number (without the wings) is used or a period is placed after the Arabic number: 5 *or* 5.

5. Outline Sequence

A period is used after the numbers and letters in an outline, unless such symbols are enclosed in parentheses. Never use an isolated number or a letter symbol such as "A," "1," "a," "(1)" etc. unless it is in a sequence.

I. ....
- A. ....
- B. ....
- C. ....
  - 1. ....
  - 2. ....
    - a. ....
    - b. ....
      - (1) ....
      - (2) ....
      - (3) ....
        - (a) ....
        - (b) ....
          - (i) ....
          - (ii) ....

II. ....
- A. ....
- B. ....
  - 1. ....
  - 2. ....
    - a. ....
    - b. ....
    - c. ....

B. BUSINESS MEETINGS AND MINUTES

Reports, minutes, memorandums, and press releases are germane to business routine. Businessmen are frequently called upon to conduct or to participate in business meetings. Whether the meeting is conducted informally or formally, a written report is made to record the proceedings of the meeting.

A secretary may be called upon to take minutes at a meeting. More often it is her task to write minutes that have been taken by the secretary of the meeting, who may either dictate the minutes to her or give her the information in draft form. In typing minutes the secretary should follow whatever style has been adopted by the company. If there is no previously set form, the following are some guidelines to acceptable styles:

1. Informal Business Meeting

An informal business meeting is called for a specific purpose. As the meeting progresses, individuals may come and go according to their interest or the voice they have in certain topics. The meeting is conducted in conversational manner rather than according to strict rules of procedure. Such meetings are for the purpose of communicating ideas rather than for making policies. Decisions are in the form of recommendations rather than resolutions. The report of the meeting is in the form of a summary; it does not describe the proceedings.

In reporting the meeting, the secretary must include some basic elements, such as the date, time, and place of the meeting, the general topic or topics of discussion, the name of the chairman and the secretary of the meeting, and the names of any persons who attended the meeting. The attendance might have been recorded on an attendance sheet, which sheet could be attached to the report of the meeting. While considerable latitude is permitted in reporting an informal meeting, the organizating of topics into categories and the grouping of pertinent information under the respective heading will produce an intelligible summary.

2. Formal Business Meeting

Ordinarily the responsibility for minutes of a formal meeting is given to the secretary of the company. Corporate minutes contain the following information:

a. Membership of group—directors or stockholders
b. Kind of meeting—regular, special, or annual
c. Date, time, and place of meeting
d. Names of persons in attendance
e. Record of proceedings of the meeting

A knowledge of parliamentary procedure will be helpful to the secretary in typing minutes of a formal meeting. The form of procedure presented below is the usual practice. In typing minutes, the title is centered at the top of the page in bold face letters. Minutes may be typed either in single or double space. A wide margin should be left on the right and left sides of the paper and also at the bottom. A backing sheet or other device should be used in order that the bottom margin on each sheet may be approximately the same. The form of parliamentary procedure is basically as follows:

1. Record of attendance
2. Minutes of previous meeting (sometimes the minutes are read orally and sometimes they are circulated before the meeting and the body approves them without an oral reading)
3. Approval of minutes
4. *Reports of Officers
5. *Reports of Standing Committees
6. *Reports of Special Committees
7. Unfinished business
8. New business
9. Appointments of committees
10. Nominations and elections
11. Date of next meeting (sometimes)
12. Adjournment

A good practice in writing minutes is to type a caption at the beginning of each new topic. This will help identify what appears in the minutes. Each resolution must be recorded exactly as given and must be typed single space in a separate indented paragraph. A resolution begins with the word RESOLVED.

RESOLVED, that. . . .

; and it was further

RESOLVED, that. . . .

; and it was further

Minutes books are important legal records and are subject to examination by auditors and by courts in their efforts to determine whether all transactions entered into by the corporation are authorized or approved in the minutes. Corporations

*Copies of reports are usually given to the Secretary of the meeting. A report may either be incorporated in the minutes or added as an addendum to the minutes.

are required by law to keep a minute book for recording minutes of meetings of directors and stockholders. Directors' meetings are held at frequent intervals, whereas stockholders usually meet once a year.

The extent of the secretary's responsibility varies from office to office. If the secretary has assisted in taking minutes at a meeting, she should first make a draft copy of the minutes and then present them to her employer for suggestions, additions, or corrections. Since minutes are legal documents, they must be accurate in every detail as to spelling of names, numerical references, and actions taken at the meeting. Minutes are always signed by the secretary of the meeting. At times, an assistant secretary or other officer or officers may also be requested to sign minutes. The original copy of the minutes with signatures thereon is placed in the minute book of the corporation. The minute book is a permanent record of the corporation.

C. PROOFREADING

In the daily work of a secretary, the task of proofreading and following proofreader's marks is practically routine procedure in revising and retyping parts of documents, reports, and written communications in general. The code of proofreader's marks is universally accepted and understood. Corrections are usually made in the margin of the draft, and the place where the correction is to be made is indicated with a caret in the proof or with other pertinent mark. Lengthy inserts may be typed or handwritten on a separate page; inserts are frequently marked with "A", "B", or "1", "2", etc.

Word-processing machines in the modern office are geared to making corrections. If such equipment is not available, the typist should attempt to confine the alterations, if possible, to one or two lines. Where a word is inserted, another word of equal length may be removed so as to avoid resetting the entire paragraph. Where high-quality duplicating processes are available, corrections, insertions or deletions are often made by "cutting and pasting" the original draft. This is a time-saving technique in the preparation of lengthy documents.

Corrections in proofs are made as follows:

PROOFREADER'S MARKS

- ^ Caret, for something left out. Insert additions.
- Delete, or take out.
- .... Retain words under which dots appear, write "stet" in margin.
- stet Let it stand.
- lc or Lower case. Line drawn through a capital means lower case.
- bf Set in bold face type
- rom Change to Roman face.
- Close up.
- ... Ellipses (If preceded by a period, use 4 dots)
- Reverse; upside down
- # Insert space.
- Insert comma.
- Insert hyphen.
- Insert period.
- :/ Insert colon.
- ;/ Insert semicolon.
- !/ Insert exclamation mark.
- ?/ Insert question mark.
- Insert apostrophe.
- Insert quotation marks.
- (/) Insert parentheses.
- Move to right.
- Move to left.
- Move up.
- Move down.
- ¶ Make paragraph.
- No ¶ No paragraph.
- Transpose words or letters.
- sp. Spell out.
- // Line up. Make lines even with other matter.
- Caps. Solid caps.
- Small caps.
- Italics.
- Query to author.
- Unevenly spaced; correct spacing.
- Insert superior figure.
- Insert inferior figure.
- [/] Insert brackets.
- wf. Wrong font.
- ***/ Insert asterisks to indicate omission of paragraph or more.

D. CAPITALS OF STATES IN THE UNITED STATES OF AMERICA

State	*Capital*
United States of America	Washington, D. C.
Alabama	Montgomery
Alaska	Juneau
Arizona	Phoenix
Arkansas	Little Rock
California	Sacramento
Colorado	Denver
Connecticut	Hartford
Delaware	Dover
Florida	Tallahassee
Georgia	Atlanta
Hawaii	Honolulu
Idaho	Boise
Illinois	Springfield
Indiana	Indianapolis
Iowa	Des Moines
Kansas	Topeka
Kentucky	Frankfort
Louisiana	Baton Rouge
Maine	Augusta
Maryland	Annapolis
Massachusetts	Boston
Michigan	Lansing
Minnesota	St. Paul
Mississippi	Jackson
Missouri	Jefferson City
Montana	Helena
Nebraska	Lincoln
Nevada	Carson City
New Hampshire	Concord
New Jersey	Trenton
New Mexico	Santa Fe
New York	Albany
North Carolina	Raleigh
North Dakota	Bismarck
Ohio	Columbus

CAPITALS OF STATES IN THE UNITED STATES OF AMERICA (cont.)

State	*Capital*
Oklahoma	Oklahoma City
Oregon	Salem
Pennsylvania	Harrisburg
Rhode Island	Providence
South Carolina	Columbia
South Dakota	Pierre
Tennessee	Nashville
Texas	Austin
Utah	Salt Lake City
Vermont	Montpelier
Virginia	Richmond
Washington	Olympia
West Virginia	Charleston
Wisconsin	Madison
Wyoming	Cheyenne

E. CANADIAN CAPITALS

Capital of Canada Ottawa

Province	*Two-Letter Abbreviation*	*Capital*
Alberta	AB	Edmonton
British Columbia	BC	Victoria
Manitoba	MB	Winnipeg
New Brunswick	NB	Fredericton
Newfoundland	NF	St. John's
Northwest Territories	NT	Yellowknife
Nova Scotia	NS	Halifax
Ontario	ON	Toronto
Prince Edward Island	PE	Charlottetown
Quebec	PQ	Quebec
Saskatchewan	SK	Regina
Yukon Territory	YT	Whitehorse
Labrador	LB	None

F. CAPITALS OF THE WORLD AND BASIC MONETARY UNIT

Country or Territory	*Capital*	*Monetary Unit*
Afghanistan	Kabul	afghani
Albania	Tirane	lek
Algeria	Algiers	dinar
Andorra	Andorra la Vella	Franc (French franc) peseta (Spanish peseta)
Angola	Luanda	escudo
Argentina	Buenos Aires	peso
Australia	Canberra	dollar
Austria	Vienna	schilling
Bahamas	Nassau	pound
Barbados	Bridgetown	East Caribbean dollar
Belgium	Brussels	franc
Bermuda	Hamilton	pound
Bhutan	Thimbu	Indian rupee
Bolivia	LaPaz	peso
Botswana	Gaberones	South African rand
Brazil	Brasilia	cruzeiro
Bulgaria	Sophia	lev (leva)
Burma	Rangoon	kyat
Burundi	Usumbura	franc
(Cambodia, formerly) now Khmer Republic	Phnom Penh	riel
Cameroon	Yaoundé	franc
Canada	Ottawa	dollar
Central African Republic	Bángui	franc
Ceylon	—	rupee
Chad	Fort-Lamy	franc
Chile	Santiago	peso
China	Peking	yuan
Colombia	Bogotá	peso
Congo, Republic of (see Zaire)	Brazzaville	franc
Costa Rica	San José	Colón (colones)
Cuba	Havana	peso
Cyprus	Nicosia	pound

CAPITALS OF THE WORLD AND BASIC MONETARY UNIT (continued)

Country or Territory	*Capital*	*Monetary Unit*
Czechoslovakia	Prague	koruna
Dahomey	Porto-Novo	franc
Denmark	Copenhagen	kroner
Dominican Republic	Santo Domingo	peso
Ecuador	Quito	sucre
Egypt	Cairo	pound
El Salvador	San Salvador	colón (colones)
Estonia	Tallin	ruble
Ethiopia	Addis Ababa	dollar (Ethiopian)
Finland	Helsinki	markka
France	Paris	franc
Gabon	Libreville	franc
Gambia	Bathurst	pound
(Germany, East) German Democratic Republic	East Berlin	ostmark
Germany, Federal Republic of	Bonn	mark
Ghana	Accra or Akkra	cedi
Great Britain	London	pound
Greece	Athens	drachma
Guam	Agana	dollar
Guatemala	Guatemala City	quetzal (quetzales)
Guinea	Conakry	franc
Guyana	Georgetown	dollar
Haiti	Port-au-Prince	gourde
Holland or Netherlands	Amsterdam; The Hague*	guilder
Honduras	Tegucigalpa	lempira
Hong Kong	Victoria	dollar
Hungary	Budapest	forint
Iceland	Reykjavik	króna (krónur)
India	New Delhi	rupee

*Amsterdam is parliamentary capital and The Hague, Permanent Court of International Justice and royal residence.

CAPITALS OF THE WORLD AND BASIC MONETARY UNIT (continued)

Country or Territory	*Capital*	*Monetary Unit*
Indonesia	Djakarta	rupiah
Iran	Tehran	rial
Iraq	Baghdad	dinar
Ireland (Eire)	Dublin	pound
Israel	Jerusalem	pound
Italy	Rome	lire
Ivory Coast	Abidjan	franc
Jamaica	Kingston	pound
Japan	Tokyo	yen
Jordan	Amman	dinar
Kenya	Nairobi	shilling
Khmer Republic (formerly Cambodia)	Phnom Penh	riel
Korea (North)	Pyongyang	won
Korea (South)	Seoul	won
Kuwait	Kuwait	dinar
Laos	Luang Prabang	kip
Latvia	Riga	ruble
Lebanon	Beirut	pound
Lesotho	Maseru	S. African rand
Liberia	Monrovia	dollar
Libya (or Libyan Arab Republic)	Tripoli & Benghazi	pound
Liechtenstein	Vaduz	franc (Swiss franc)
Lithuania	Vilnius	ruble
Luxembourg	Arlon	franc
Macao	Macao	pataca
Madagascar (Now Malagasy Republic)		
Madeira	Funchal	escudo
Malagasy Republic	Tananarive	franc
Malawai (formerly Nyasaland)	Zomba	pound

CAPITALS OF THE WORLD AND BASIC MONETARY UNIT (continued)

Country or Territory	*Capital*	*Monetary Unit*
Malaya, Federation of (Now a territory of the Federation of Malaysia)	Kuala Lumpur	dollar
Malaysia, Federation of	Kuala Lumpur	dollar
Maldives, Republic of	Maldives	rupee
Mali	Bamako	franc
Malta	Valletta	pound
Mauritania	Nouakchott	franc
Mauritius	Port Louis	rupee
Mexico, Republic of in Federal District	Mexico City	peso
Mexico, Central	Toluca	peso
Monaco	Monaco	franc (French franc)
Morocco, French	Rabat	dirham
Mozambique	Lourenco Marques	escudo
Muscat and Oman (See Oman)	Muscat	Gulf rupee
Nepal	Katmandu	rupee
Netherlands or Holland	Amsterdam; The Hague	guilder (florin)
Netherlands Antilles (Dutch West Indies)	Willemstad	guilder (florin)
New Caledonia	Nouméa	franc
New Zealand	Wellington	dollar
Nicaragua	Managua	córdoba
Niger	Niamey	franc
Nigeria	Lagos	pound
Norway	Oslo	kroner
Oman and Muscat (See Muscat)	Muscat	Gulf rupee

CAPITALS OF THE WORLD AND BASIC MONETARY UNIT (continued)

Country or Territory	*Capital*	*Monetary Unit*
Pakistan	Islamabad	rupee
Panama	Panama City	balboa
Paraquay	Asunción	guaranî (guaranîes)
Peru	Lima	sol (soles)
Philippines (Republic of the Philippines)	Manila—Quezon City	peso
Poland	Warsaw	zloty
Portugal	Lisbon	escudo
Puerto Rico	San Juan	U.S. dollar
Rhodesia (formerly Southern Rhodesia)	Salisbury	pound
Roumania	Bucharest	leu
Russia	Moscow	ruble
Rwanda	Kigali	franc
San Marino	San Marino	lira (lire)
Sarawak	Kuching	dollar
Saudi Arabia	Riyadh	riyal
Senegal	Dakar	franc
Sierra Leone	Freetown	leone
Singapore	Singapore	dollar
Somalia or Somali Republic	Mogadishu	shilling
Somaliland, French	Ogaden	franc
South Africa, Republic of	(Administrative) Pretoria (Legislative) Capetown (Judicial) Bloemfontein	rand
Spain	Madrid	peseta
Sudan	Khartoum	pound
Surinam	Paramaribo	guilder (florin)
Sweden	Stockholm	kroner

CAPITALS OF THE WORLD AND BASIC MONETARY UNIT (continued)

Country or Territory	*Capital*	*Monetary Unit*
Switzerland	Bern	franc
Syria	(Administrative) Beirut (Legislative) Damascus	pound
Tahiti	Papeete	franc
Tanganyika	Dar es Salaam	shilling
Tanzania E. Africa	Dar es Salaam	shilling
[republic East Africa formed in 1964 by union of Tanganyika and Zanzibar]		
Thailand	Bangkok	baht
Tobago & Trinidad	Port of Spain	dollar
Togo, Republic of (West Africa)	Lomé	franc
Tonga	Nukualofa	pound
Trinidad & Tobago	Port of Spain	dollar
Tunisia	Tunis	dinar
Turkey	Ankara	lira
Uganda	Kampala	shilling
United Arab Emirates	Abu Dhabi	pound
United Kingdom of Great Britain and Northern Ireland	London	pound
United States of America	Washington, D. C.	dollar
Upper Volta	Ouagadougou	franc
Uruguay	Montevideo	peso
U.S.S.R. (Russia)	Moscow	ruble
Venezuela	Caracas	bolivar
Vietnam, North	Hanoi	
Vietnam, South	Saigon	piaster
Virgin Islands	Charlotte Amalie	dollar

CAPITALS OF THE WORLD AND BASIC MONETARY UNIT (Continued)

Country or Territory	*Capital*	*Monetary Unit*
Western Samoa	Apia	Australian dollar
Yemen Arab Republic	San'a	imadi—Maria Teresa thaler
Yemen, Southern (or People's Democratic Republic of Yemen)	Aden	shilling
Yucatan	Mérida	peso
Yugoslavia	Belgrade	dinar
Zaire (formerly Republic of the Congo; formerly Belgian Congo)	Kinshasa	franc
Zambia	Lusaka	pound

G. WORLD INFORMATION

1. Dimensions of the Continents

Asia	17,000,000 square miles
Africa	11,500,000 square miles
North America	8,000,000 square miles
South America	6,800,000 square miles
Polar Regions	6,205,000 square miles
Oceania	4,000,000 square miles
Europe	3,750,000 square miles

2. Arabic Figures and Roman Numerals

1	I	i	30	XXX	xxx
2	II	ii	40	XL	xl
3	III	iii	50	L	l
4	IV	iv	60	LX	lx
5	V	v	70	LXX	lxx
6	VI	vi	80	LXXX	lxxx
7	VII	vii	90	XC	xc
8	VIII	viii	100	C	c
9	IX	ix	200	C	cc
10	X	x	300	CCC	ccc
11	XI	xi	400	CCCC or CD	cd or cccc
12	XII	xii	500	D	d
13	XIII	xiii	600	DC	dc
14	XIV	xiv	900	CM	cx
15	XV	xv	1,000	M	m
16	XVI	xvi	2,000	MM	mm
17	XVII	xvii	2,500	MMD	mmd
18	XVIII	xviii	5,000	$\overline{V}$*	
19	XIX	xix	10,000	$\overline{X}$*	
20	XX	xx			

Note: A letter placed after a Roman numeral of greater value indicates addition; a letter placed before a Roman numeral of greater value indicates subtraction.

*A line over a numeral multiplies the value by 1,000; thus,

$\overline{L}$ = 50,000
$\overline{C}$ = 100,000
$\overline{D}$ = 500,000
$\overline{M}$ = 1,000,000
$\overline{MDC}$ = 1,600,000

H. THE METRIC SYSTEM

1. Implications

The metric system, a decimal system, is also known as the International System of Units (S.I.). It is in use by more than eighty percent of the world's population in countries in which the metric system is either firmly established or conversion to the system is in process.

Legislation pending in the Congress of the United States for more than a decade culminated in the Metric Conversion Act of 1975, when President Ford signed P.L. 94-168 on December 23, 1975. This Act led to the creation of the United States Metric Board, composed of 17 members representing industry, education, science, engineering, and the public at large. While the Metric Conversion Act provides official government support of the conversion, it does not stipulate a specific time within which conversion must be accomplished. The Act calls for voluntary conversion, which implies that each segment of the economy may adopt the metric system when such conversion will best serve its interest.

The metric system will affect business and industry, particularly manufacturing, labor, accounting, science and engineering. It will have a strong impact on mathematics and on mathematics-oriented business subjects. The individual consumer is gradually being introduced to the practical awareness of the effects of the new measuring system in daily living, with more than half of our canned goods labeled in both metric and standard (English) measure. Many states have constructed new highway signs showing distances in both kilometers and miles.

In the field of education, plans are being made for the implementation of the metric system in the learning process in the school system and many states plan to convert textbooks to the metric system between 1980 and 1984. The change to the metric system will be gradual, not abrupt.

2. Units of the Metric System

The metric system is a logically planned system. Its decimal basis conforms to the numeration system presently in use. The meter, which is the basic metric unit of length, is international in character. About ten units of the metric system are in use in everyday life. The fundamental units of the metric system are as follows:

a. Basic Units

Unit of *length*	= *meter*	= about 1.1 yards (a little longer than a yard)
Unit of *capacity*	= *liter*=	= about 1.06 quarts (liquid); 0.9 quarts (dry)
Unit of *weight*	= *gram*	= 0.03527 oz. (about the weight of a paper clip)

b. Common Prefixes

The following *common prefixes* are used with the basic units:

milli	= 0.001	(one-thousandth)
centi	= 0.01	(one-hundredth)
kilo	= 1000	(one-thousand times)

c. Commonly Used Units

mm	millimeter	0.001 meter
cm	centimeter	0.01 meter
km	kilometer	1,000 meters
ml	milliliter	0.001 liter
kg	kilogram	1,000 grams
h	hectare	2½ acres
t	tonne	about one ton
C	Celsius	degrees in temperature (e.g. 37 degrees Celsius = 98.6 degrees Fahrenheit)

d. Metric Terms, Symbols and Equivalents

(1) *Length or Linear Measure*

Unit	*Abbreviation*	*Approximate U. S. Equivalent*
myriameter	mym	6.2 miles
kilometer	km	0.62 mile
hectometer	hm	109.36 yards
dekameter	dam	32.81 feet
meter	m	39.37 inches

Unit	*Abbreviation*	*Approximate U. S. Equivalent*
decimeter	dm	3.94 inches
centimeter	cm	0.39 inch
millimeter	mm	0.04 inch

(2) *Volume Measure*

dekastere	das	13.10 cubic yards
stere	s	1.31 cubic yards
decistere	ds	3.53 cubic feet
cubic centimeter	cu cm *or* cm³ *or* cc	0.061 cubic inch

(3) *Capacity Measure*

Unit	*Abbre-viation*	*Approximate U. S. Equivalent* *Cubic*	*Dry*	*liquid*
kiloliter	kl	1.31 cu. yards		
hectoliter	hl	3.53 cu. feet	2.84 bushels	
dekaliter	dal	0.35 cu. foot	1.14 pecks	2.64 gallons
liter	l	61.02 cu. inches	0.908 quart	1.057 quarts
deciliter	dl	6.1 cu. inches	0.18 pint	0.21 pint
centiliter	cl	0.6 cu. inch		0.338 fluid-ounce
milliliter	ml	0.06 cu. inch		0.27 fluid-ram

(4) *Mass and Weight Measure*

metric ton	MT *or* t	1.1 tons
quintal	q	220.46 pounds
kilogram	kg	2.2046 pounds
hectogram	hg	3.527 ounces
dekagram	dag	0.353 ounce
gram	g *or* gm	0.035 ounce
decigram	dg	1.543 grains
centigram	cg	0.154 grain
milligram	mg	0.015 grain

(5) *Area Measure*

square kilometer	sq km *or* km^2	0.3861 square mile
hectare	ha	2.47 acres
are	a	119.60 square yards
centare	ca	10.76 square feet
square centimeter	sq cm *or* cm^2	0.155 square inch

In summary, the basic units are:

meter	little longer than a yard
kilometer	0.62 mile
centimeter	0.39 inch
liter	little more than a quart
gram	about the weight of a paper clip
kilogram	2 pounds +

e. Decimal and Metric System

Numeral	*Decimal*	*Metric*	*Symbol*
1,000 times	thousands	kilo	k
100 times	hundreds	hecto	h
10 times	tens	deka	da
1	ones	unit	"I"
1/10 (0.1)	one-tenth	deci	d
1/100 (0.01)	one-hundredth	centi	c
1/1000 (0.001)	one-thousandth	milli	m

The metric conversion carries far-reaching implications for all areas of business and consumer use. Substitution of metric units for customary (English) units will be provided in references, labeling, measurements, publications, communications, and charts. In fact, all metric unit changes in consumer items, regardless of whatever hardware conversions were necessary in the manufacturing area, will be soft conversions so far as the consumer is concerned because to the consumer it will simply mean a change in terminology.

SUMMARY

Chapter 10 contains pertinent information relating to various facets of report writing with footnotes and bibliography. Particular attention is given to the format of minutes both for informal and formal business meetings, together with a list of proofreader's marks. This chapter also presents a list of capitals of the United States and capitals of the world, along with information relating to dimensions of continents, and Arabic figures and Roman numerals. Also included is an outline of the Metric System consisting of basic metric units, common prefixes, metric terms, symbols, and equivalents.

INDEX